Welcome to this journey of healing.
It will be full of colours, peace and growth.
Research showed that mindfulness and meditation have a huge impact on the brain neural activity. This, in turn, affects health on many levels: it improves the immune system, it helps the regulation of hormones, it improves stress response, it regulates the production of the insulin-like growth factor (IGF)-I and of the brain-derived neurotrophic factor (BDNF) among the others.
In particular (IGF)-I plays an important role in childhood growth and has a tissues-repairing effect in adult, while (BDNF), found in mammals' brains, is involved in neuroplasticity and makes the difference between a healthy and a pathological brain. The list of physical factors affected by mindfulness practices can go on for pages. Here, it is enough to keep in mind that mindfulness shape the neural activity, for the better.
Today we know that the Cartesian mind-body dualism is simply wrong. The mind and the body are "one and the same thing", to quote the philosopher Spinoza.
Modern Biology, Neuroscience and Medicine all agree on the evidence of a unified framework expressed by the following equation

$$\text{Healthy Body} = \text{Healthy Brain}$$

We are used to read this equation from left to right, thinking that if we take enough care of our body, our brain will be healthy as well. That is absolutely true but, in the last decades, we discovered that the right-to-left reading of the equation holds true too: a healthy brain gives us a healthy body. This means that we can tap into our mind to modify our brain and thus our body. With the right techniques and tools we can literally heal our body. This book is one of those tools.

One of the major key for a good life is investing time in personal growth. We live in an era where access to the information is easier than ever before in mankind history. With a couple of clicks you can get answers on almost any subject you desire or get the books/videos/podcasts which contain the information. This sounds like magic, doesn't it? Experts in any field spend a lifetime to gather the knowledge and you can get the same beneficial effects in a couple of hours by listening to them reading their books. Magical!

The major threat to a healthy and wealthy life is you not trying to improve yourself.

All this requires time and efforts. The question is: there exists a way to combine the beneficial role of meditation with the transformative power of personal growth for people who just want to relax?

The answer is the book in your hands. It will help you to heal your soul.

Here is my definition of the soul

Soul = Body + Mind + Growth

I call the soul the union of the body and the mind in a constant search for growth. We found that you can "exercise" while relaxing and still grow and cope with stressors that inevitably show up in your daly life. We created a mandala colouring book tailored for you to help you healing your soul: few relaxing actions will make the job.

Take your favourites coloured pencils. Find a place where you can be alone, preferably. Pick one of the hundred mandala, read the associated phrase and start colouring. While you do it, it is important that you focus only on two things: the pleasure of seeing colours coming into life and the phrase you just read. Try to visualise the applications and implications. In which aspect of your life can it have the major influence? What can you change? What can be done better? What does it mean to you? What benefits you would get if you implement that concept and start taking action?

Sometimes visual connection between the shape of the drawing and the phrase will pop into your head. That is a good sign, it means you will retain the content and meaning of the phrase for long time in your neural network, i.e. your memory will be stronger when it comes to that teaching. If it does not happen, do not worry just enjoy the process. After a dozens of finished mandala you should start feeling more peaceful, grateful, relaxed, and see new opportunities in your daily life.

There is no "right way" to use the book but I give you the following advise. Finish one (or two) mandala per day, everyday for at least 21 days (the average time required for consistent changes). After that, see what happened, check your state of being and observe yourself form a higher perspective: are you still defeated by daily stressors? Or do you handle them better? Have you grown in any direction?

Later, you can start another 21-days session to reinforce the new habit. Then observe yourself again, learn to be an observer: that is the essential of mindfulness.

Use the rest of the drawings when you feel the need to heal.

I hope this will serve you well and leave a positive mark in your precious soul; now, colour-heal it.

Yours,

Dr. *Klaus N. C. Magnus*

The best way to start is to just start.

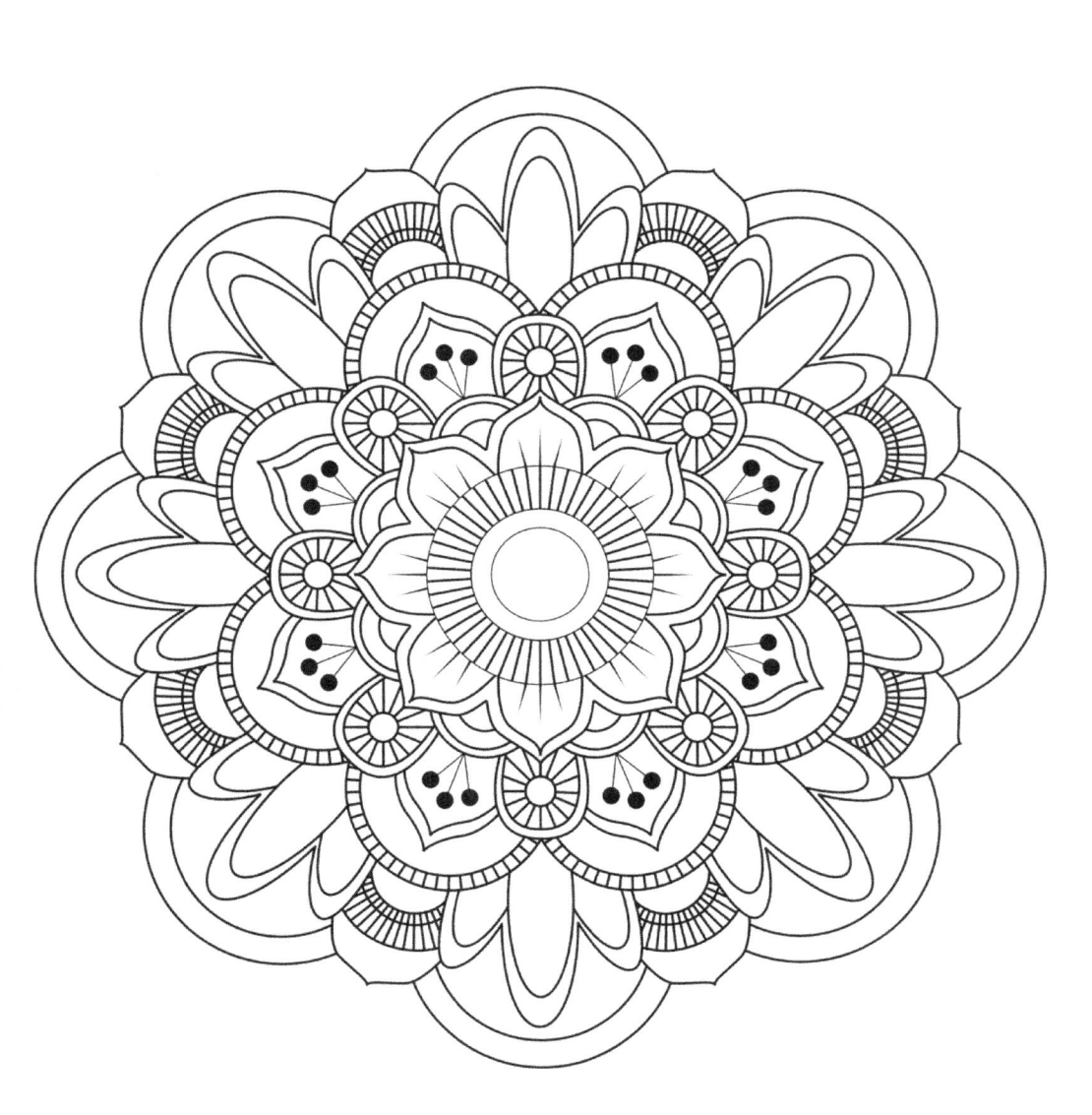

Become sophisticated.

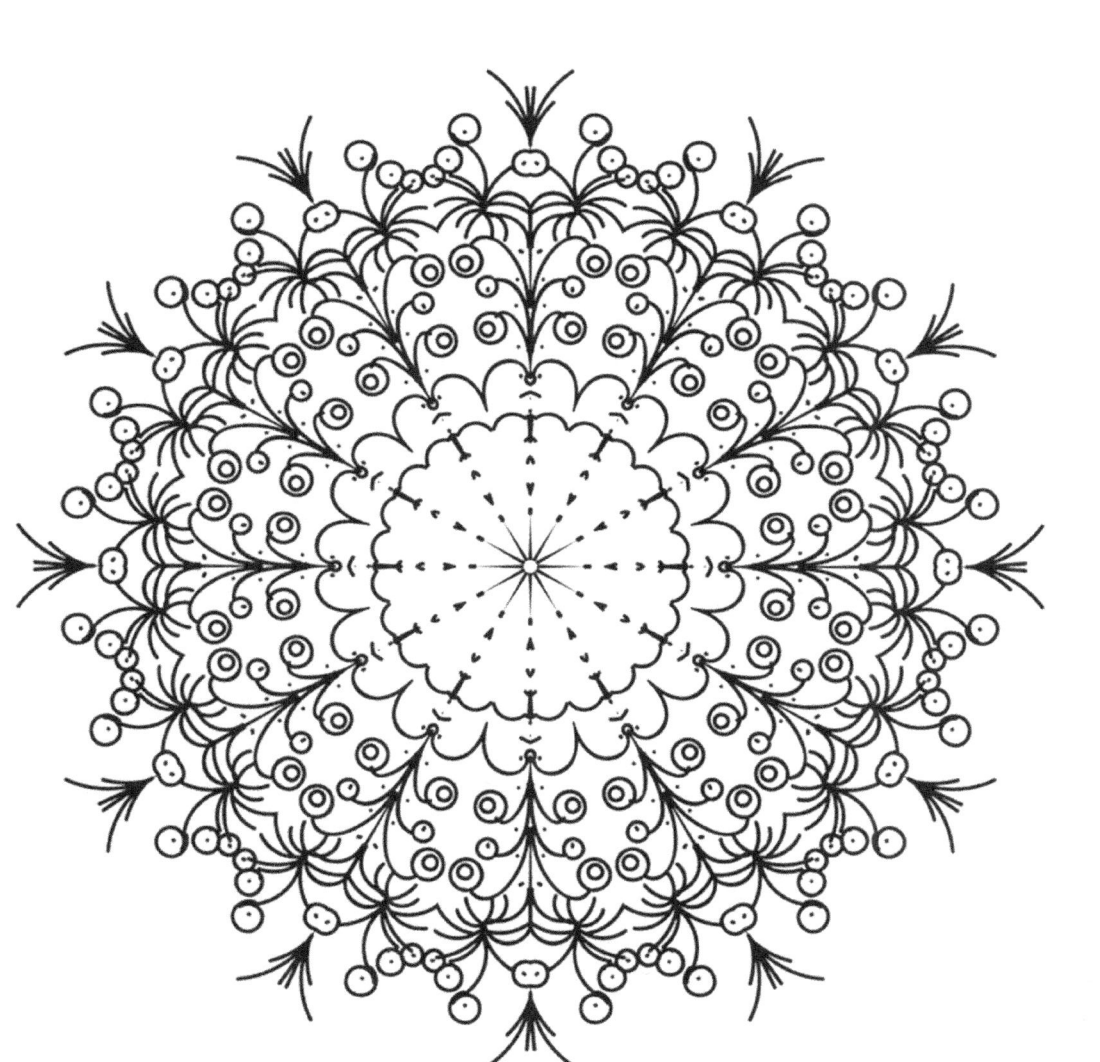

Look around, you can find hidden opportunities.

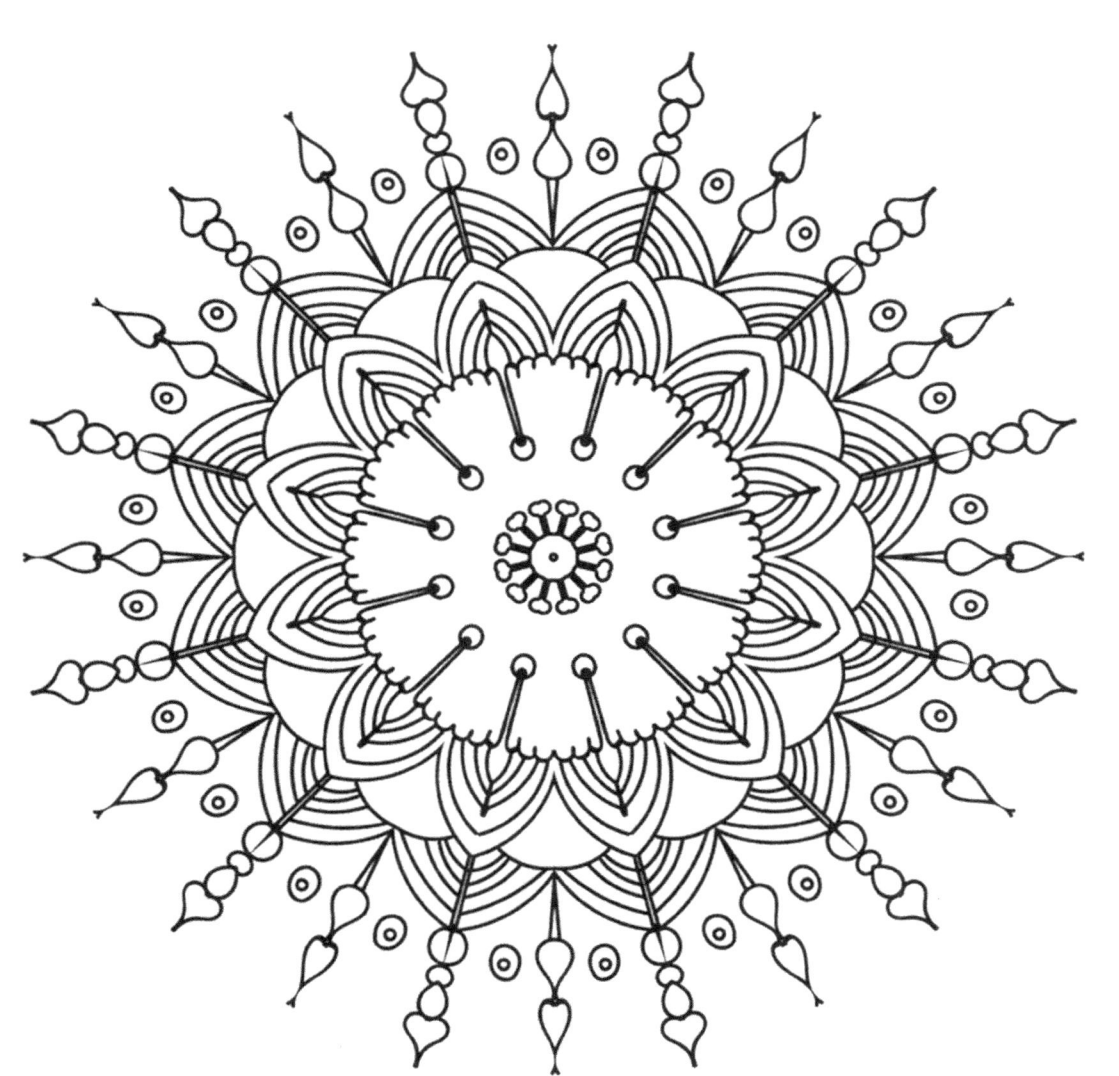

You can move while going back and forth.

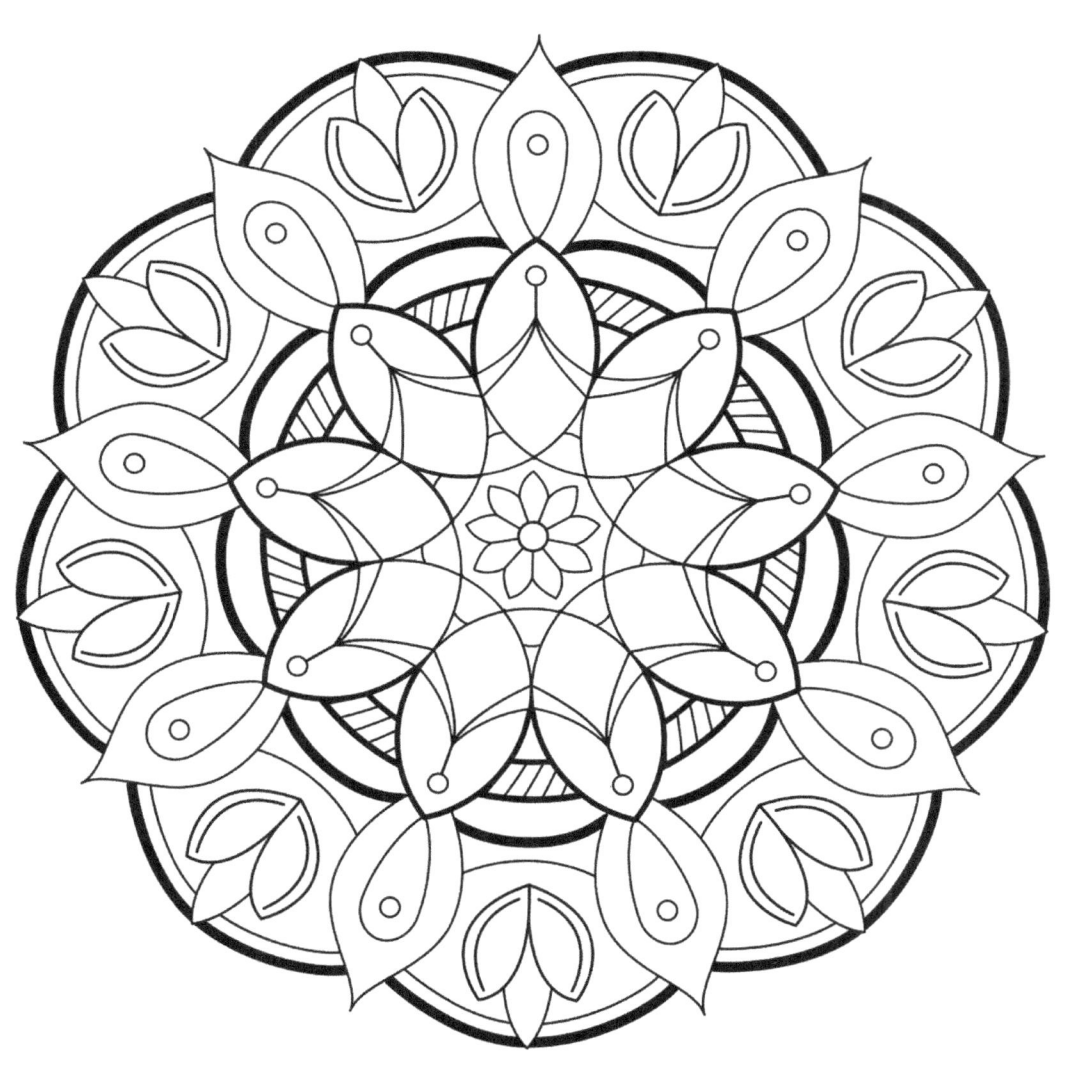

Learn to radiate positive energy.

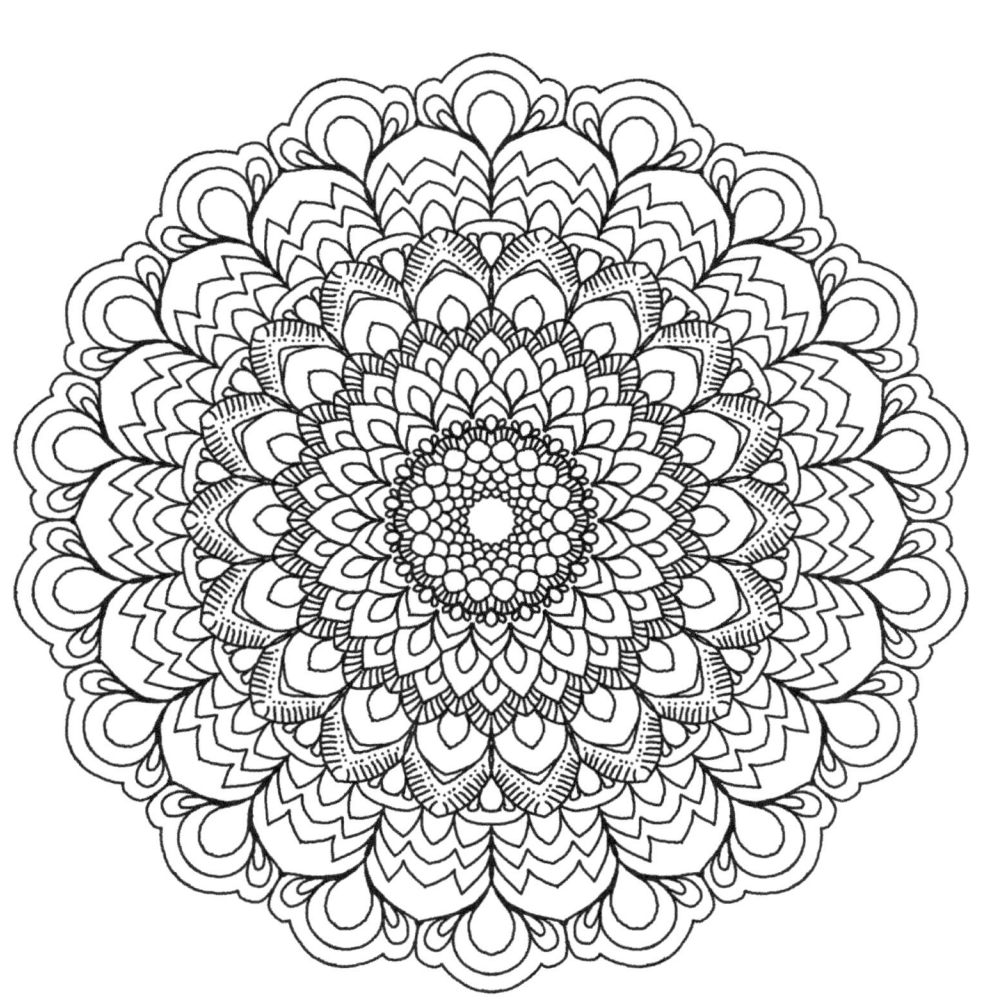

Surprise yourself doing impossible things everyday.

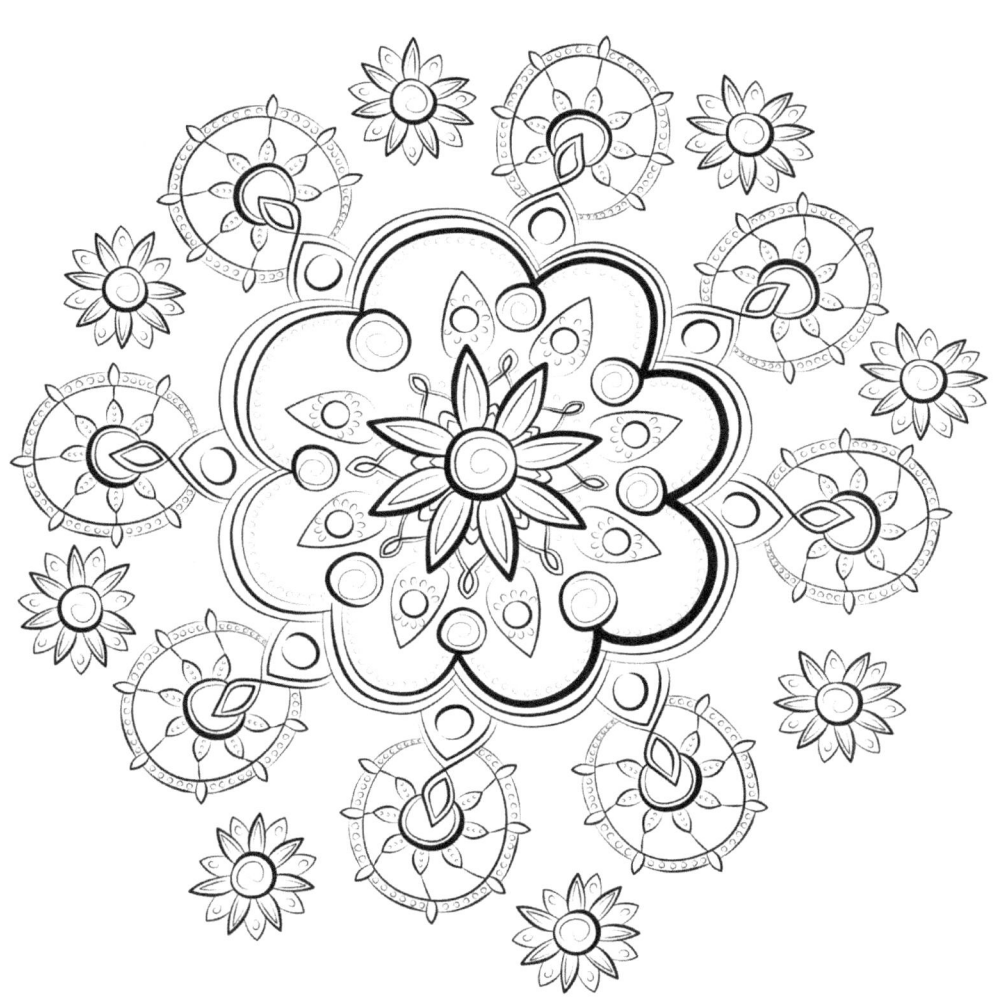

Courage is doing things despite fear.

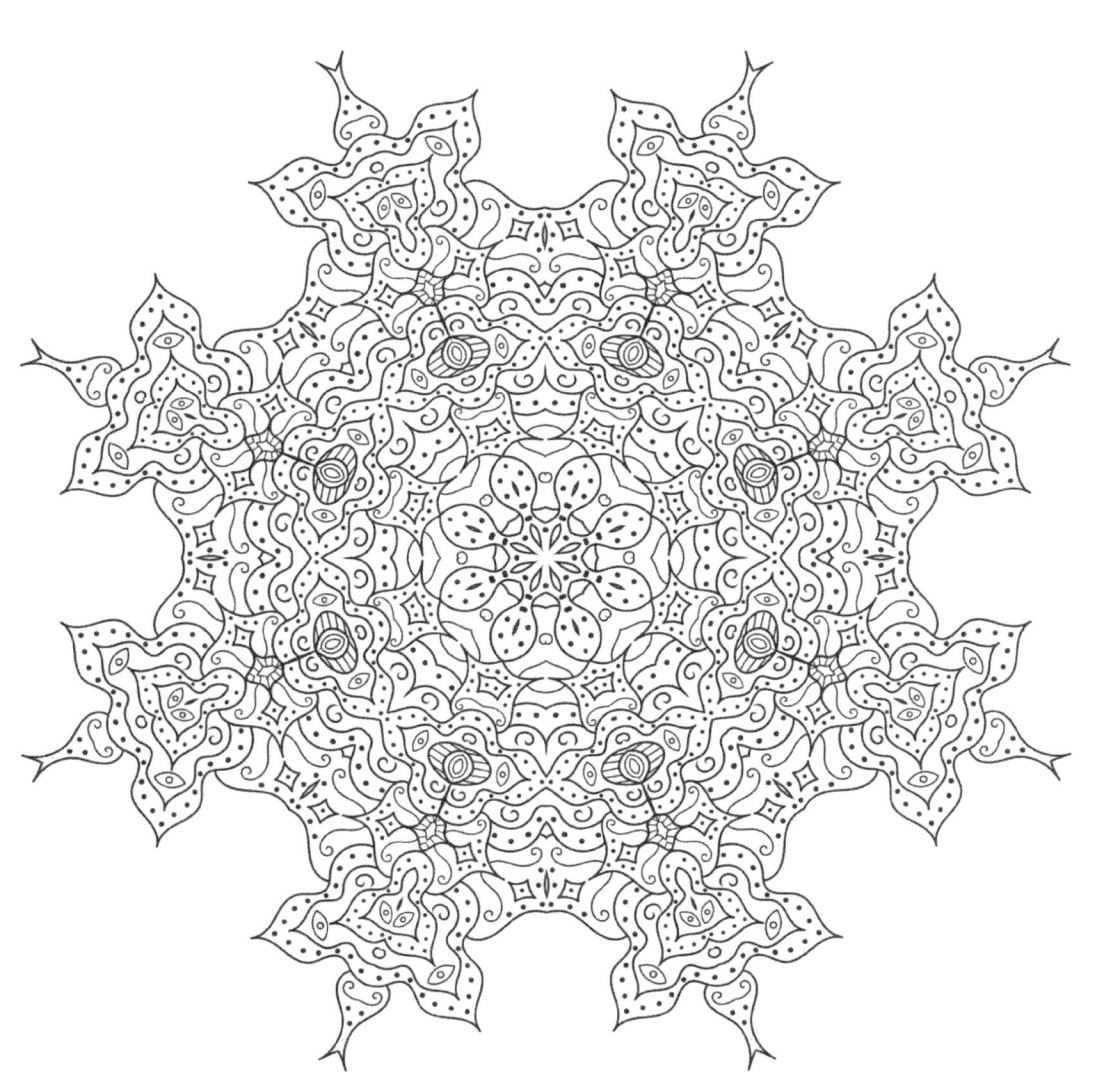

Put your life in order.

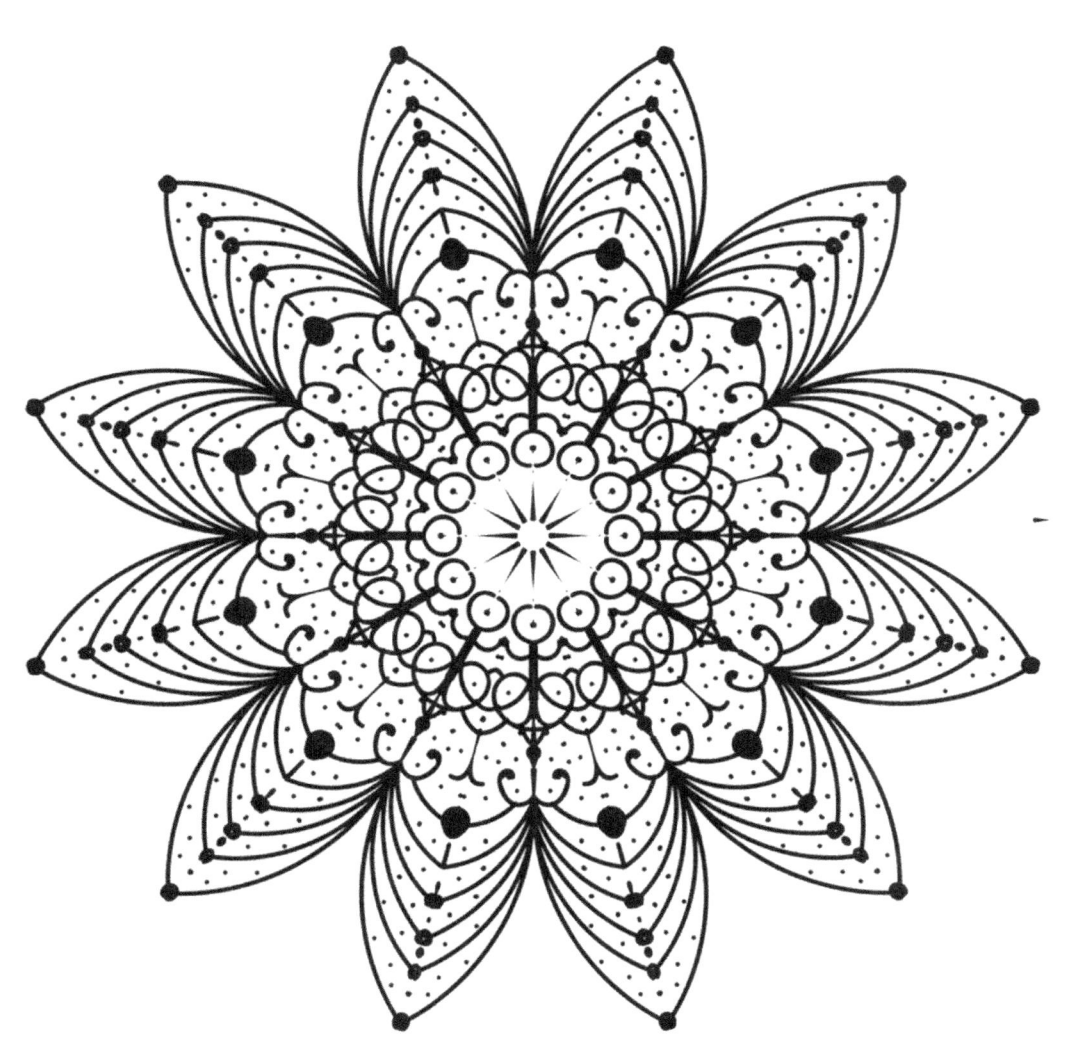

Life is circular: you get what you give.

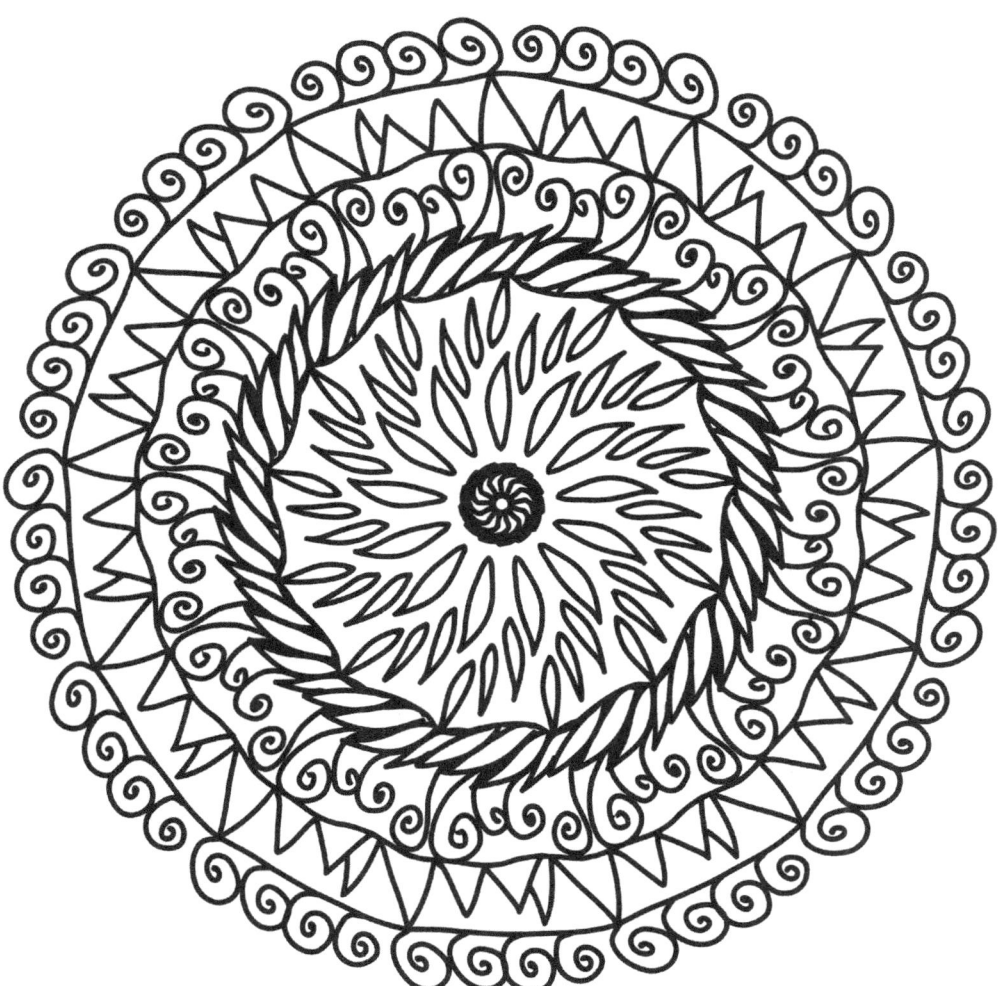

Go anywhere to discover new things.

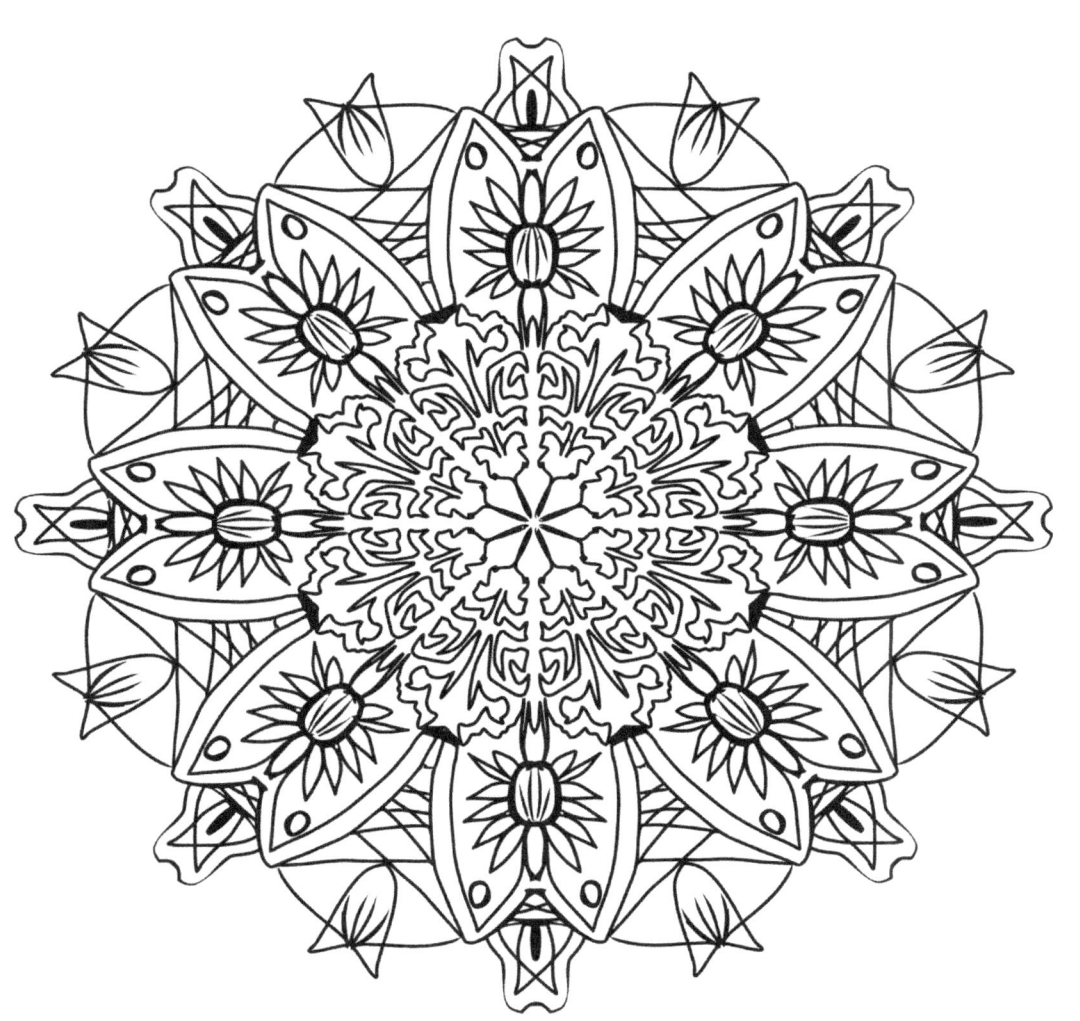

Follow your sun.

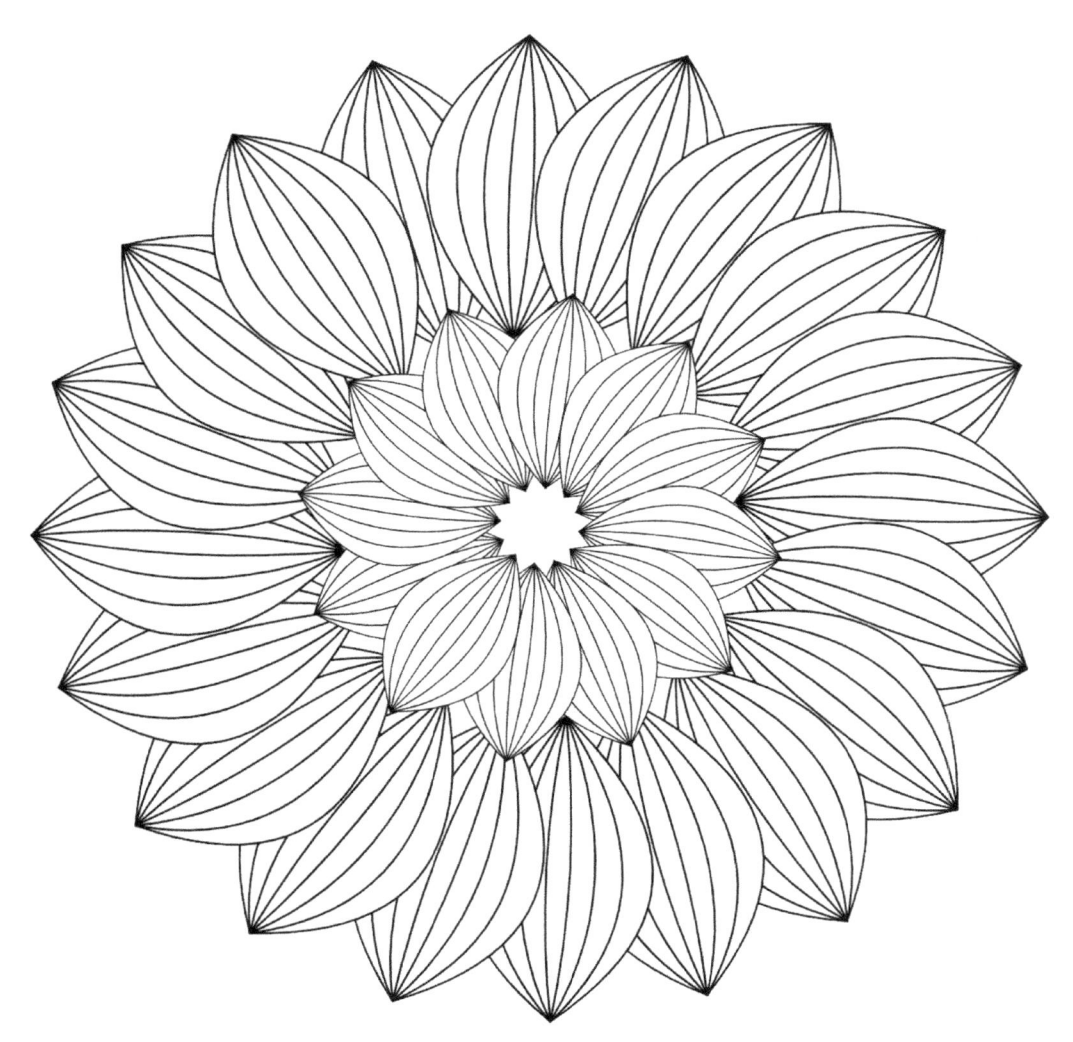

Crown your efforts with success.

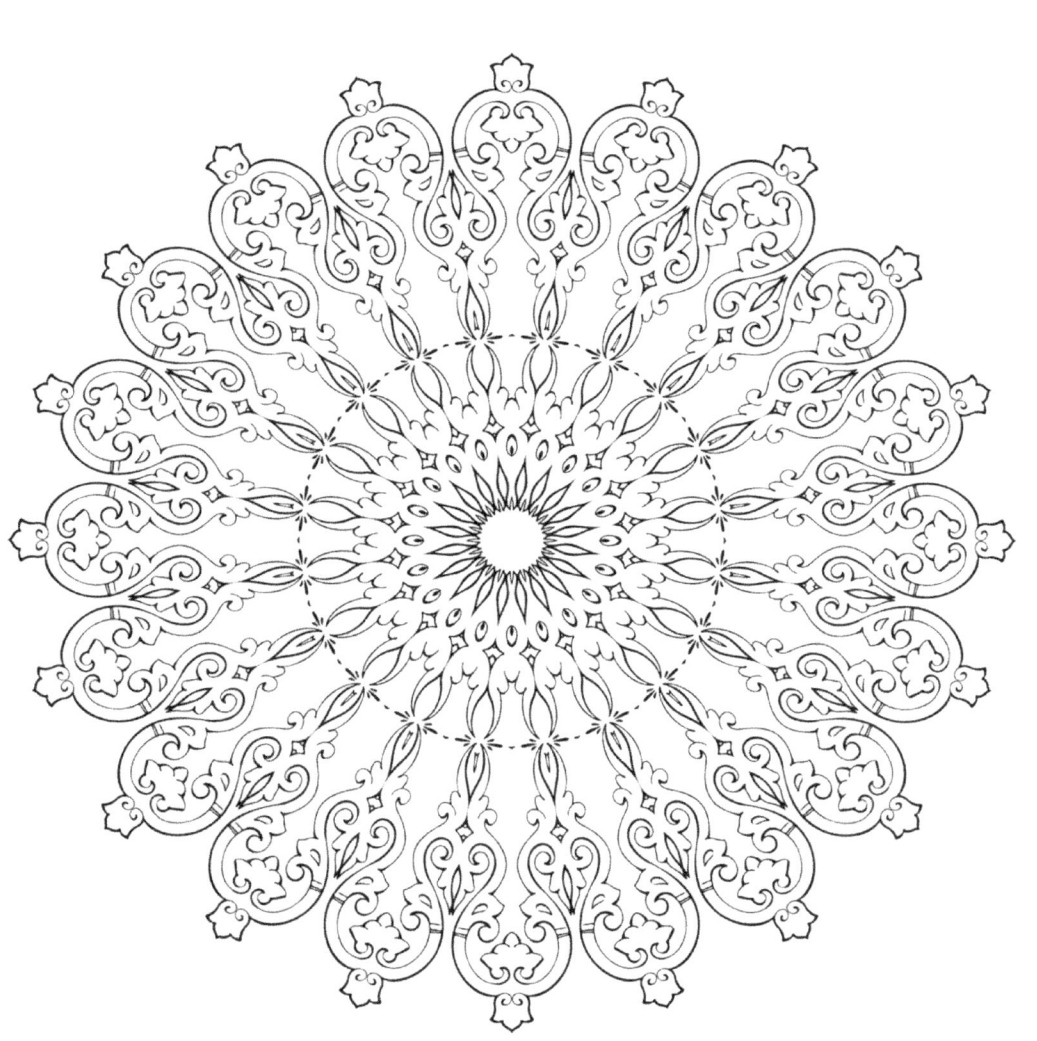

Life has different shades, accept them.

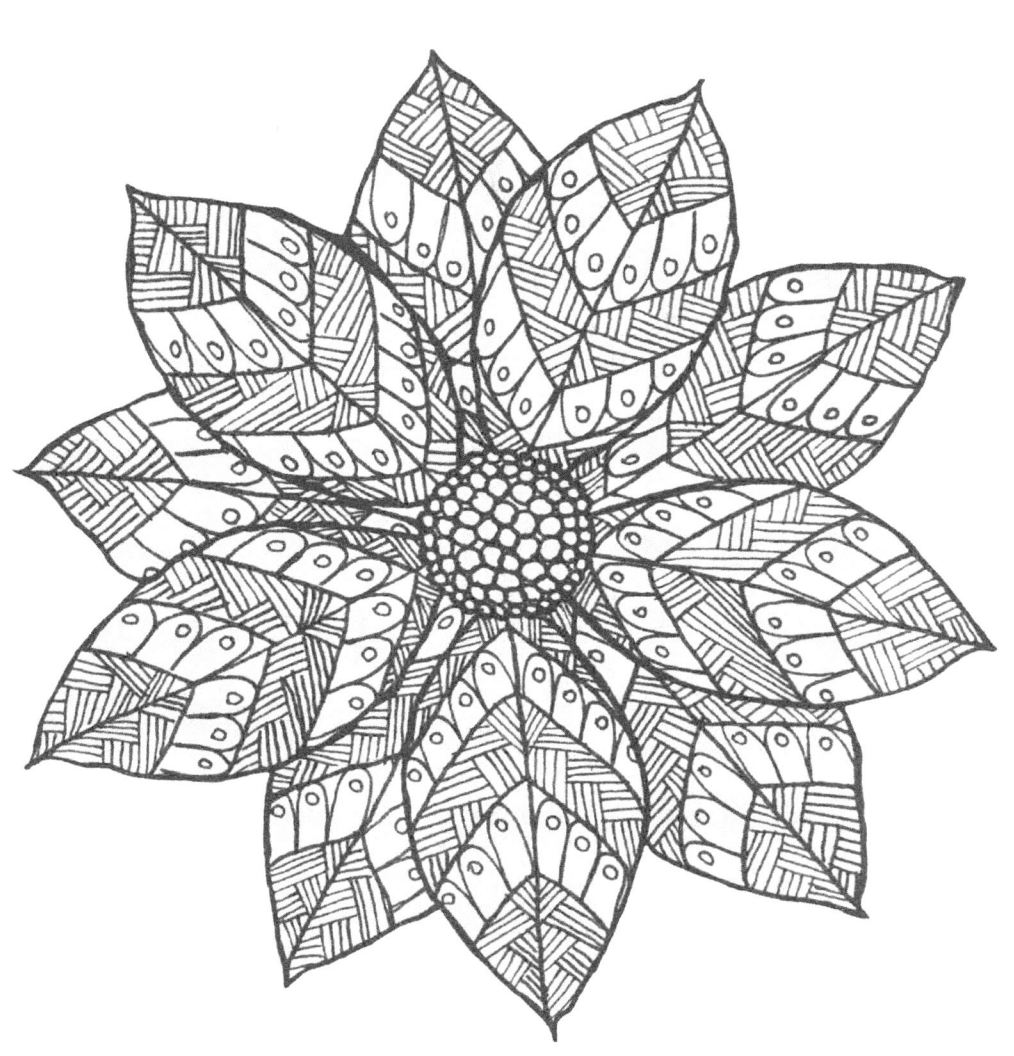

When it comes to healthy living, you will find different levels; nourish all of them.

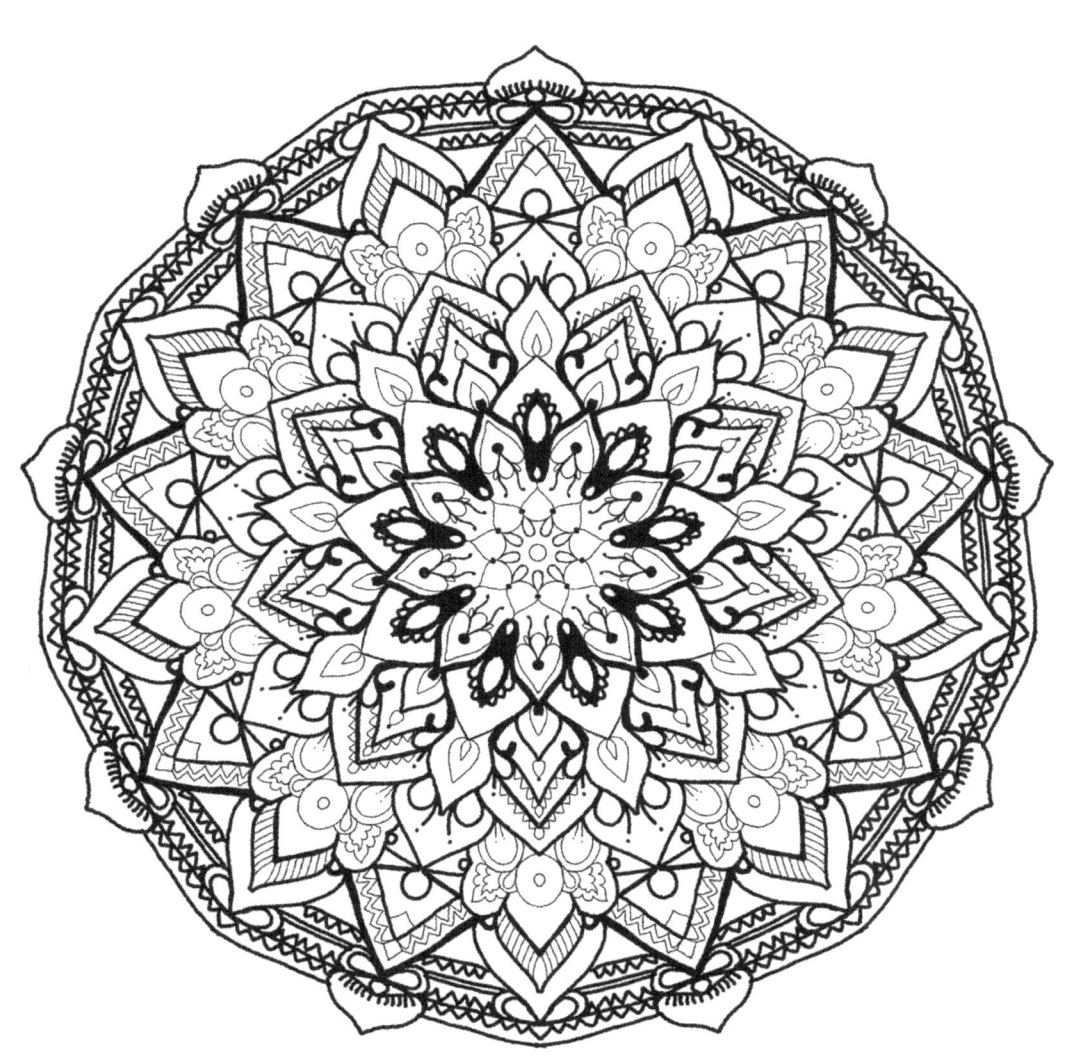

Get closer to Nature.

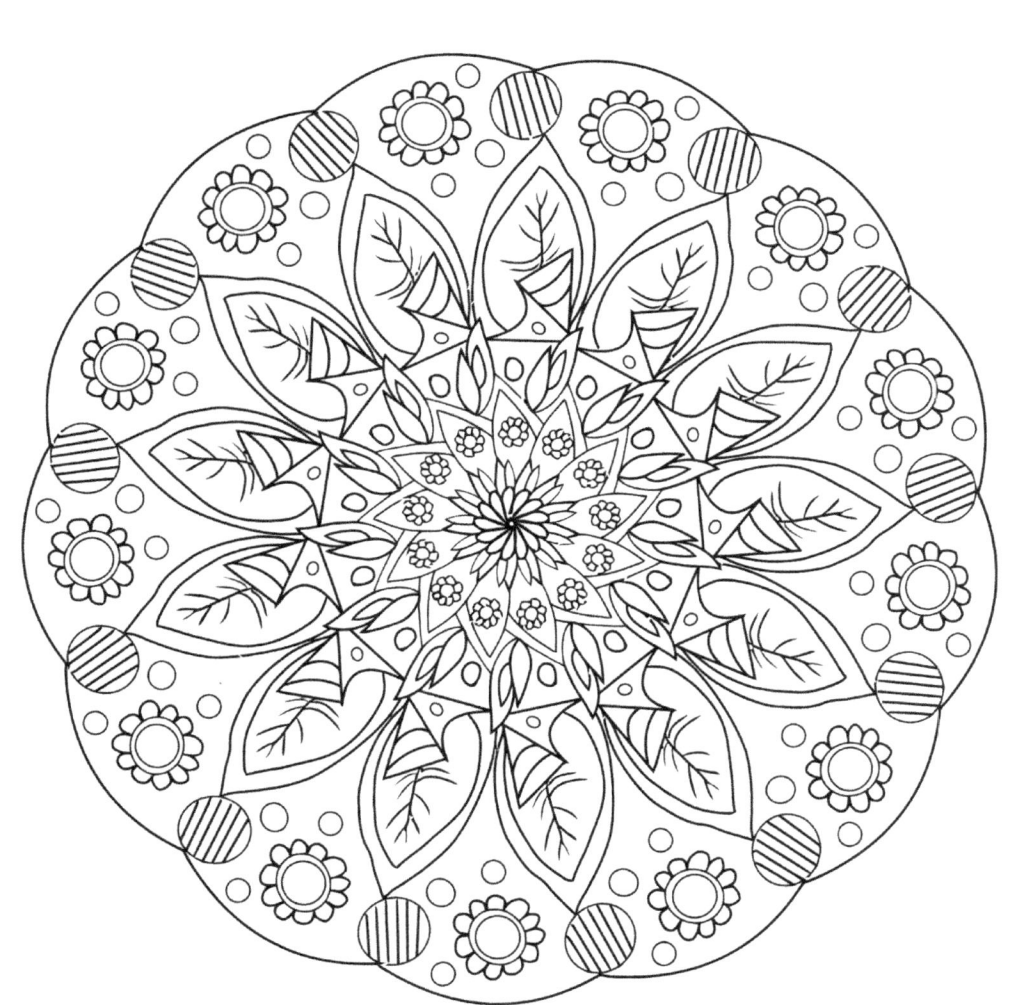

If you cannot see, try again.

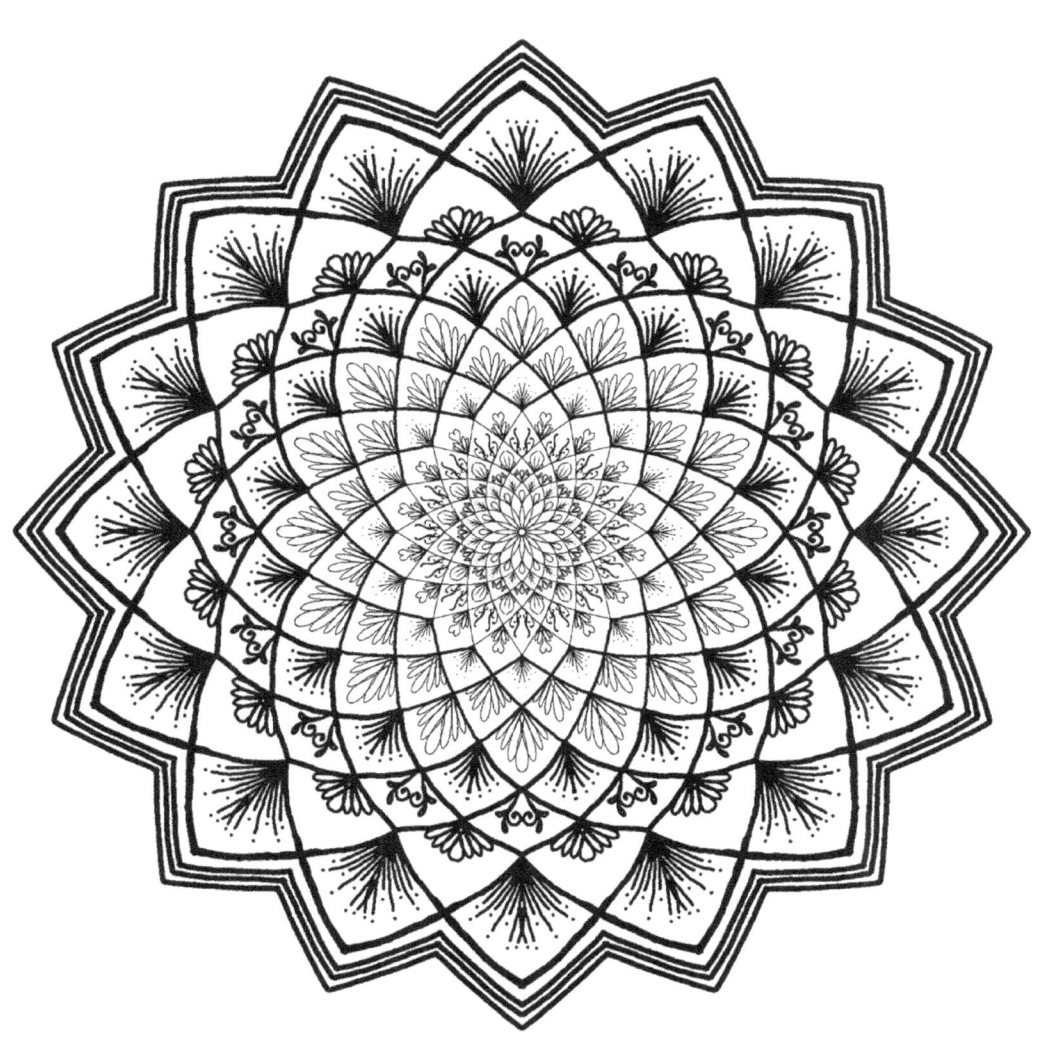

It's all about balance.

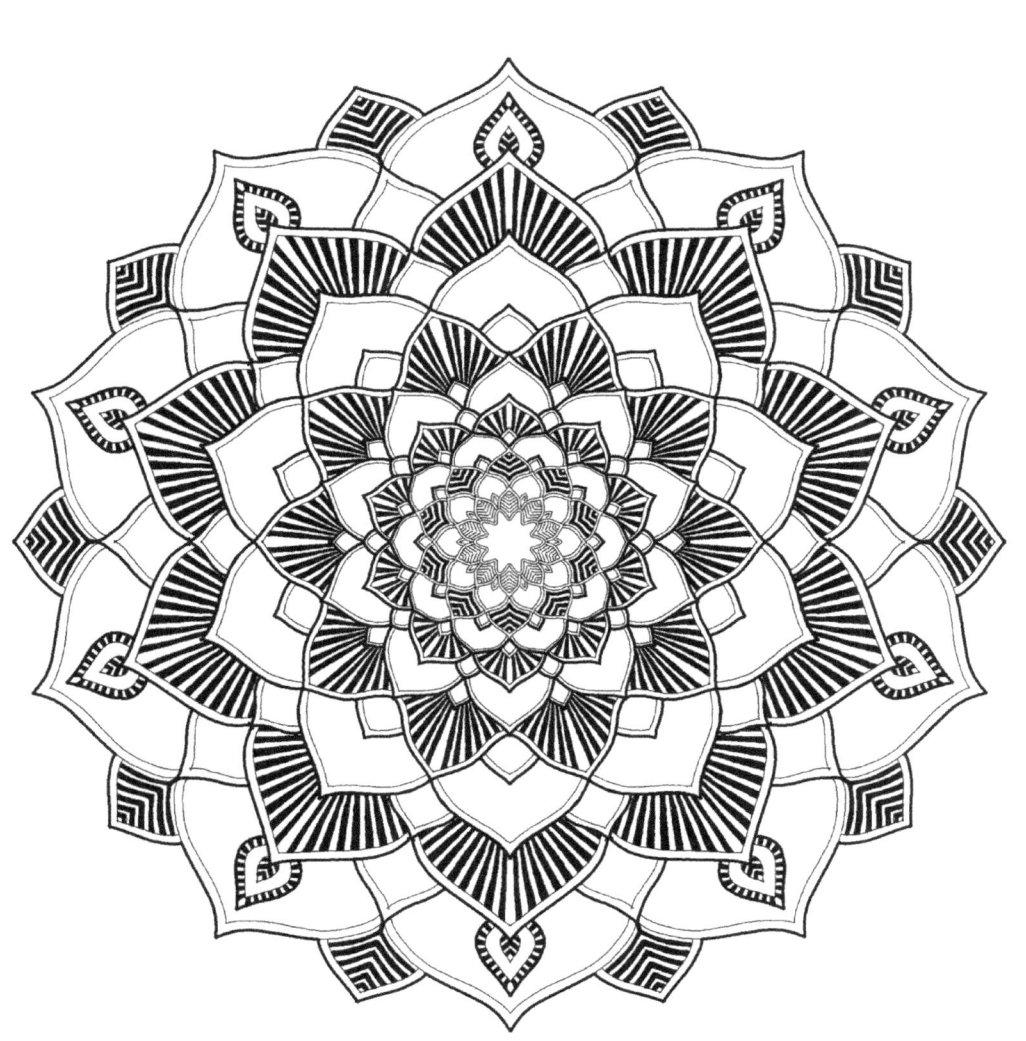

Take it easy.

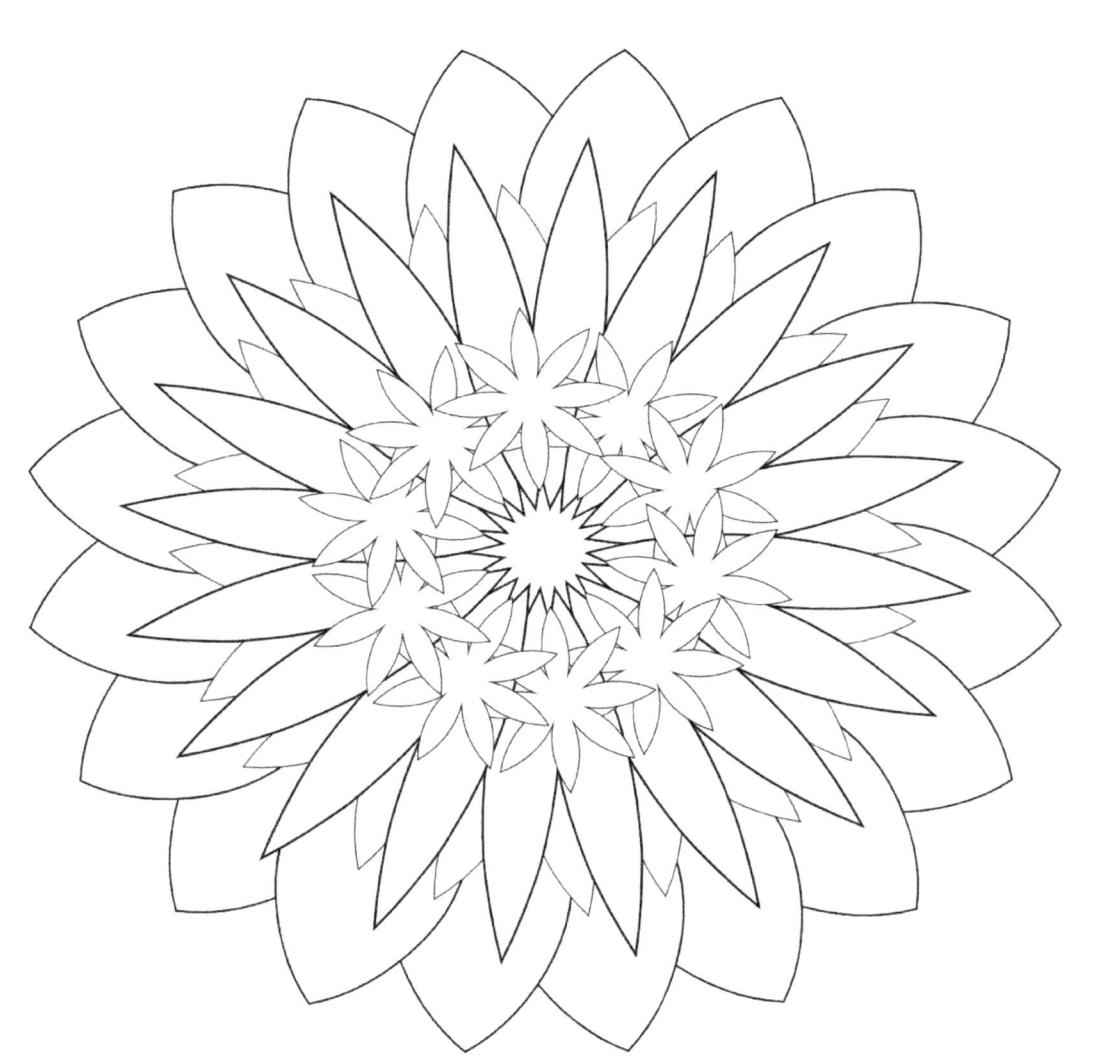

Go to the point.

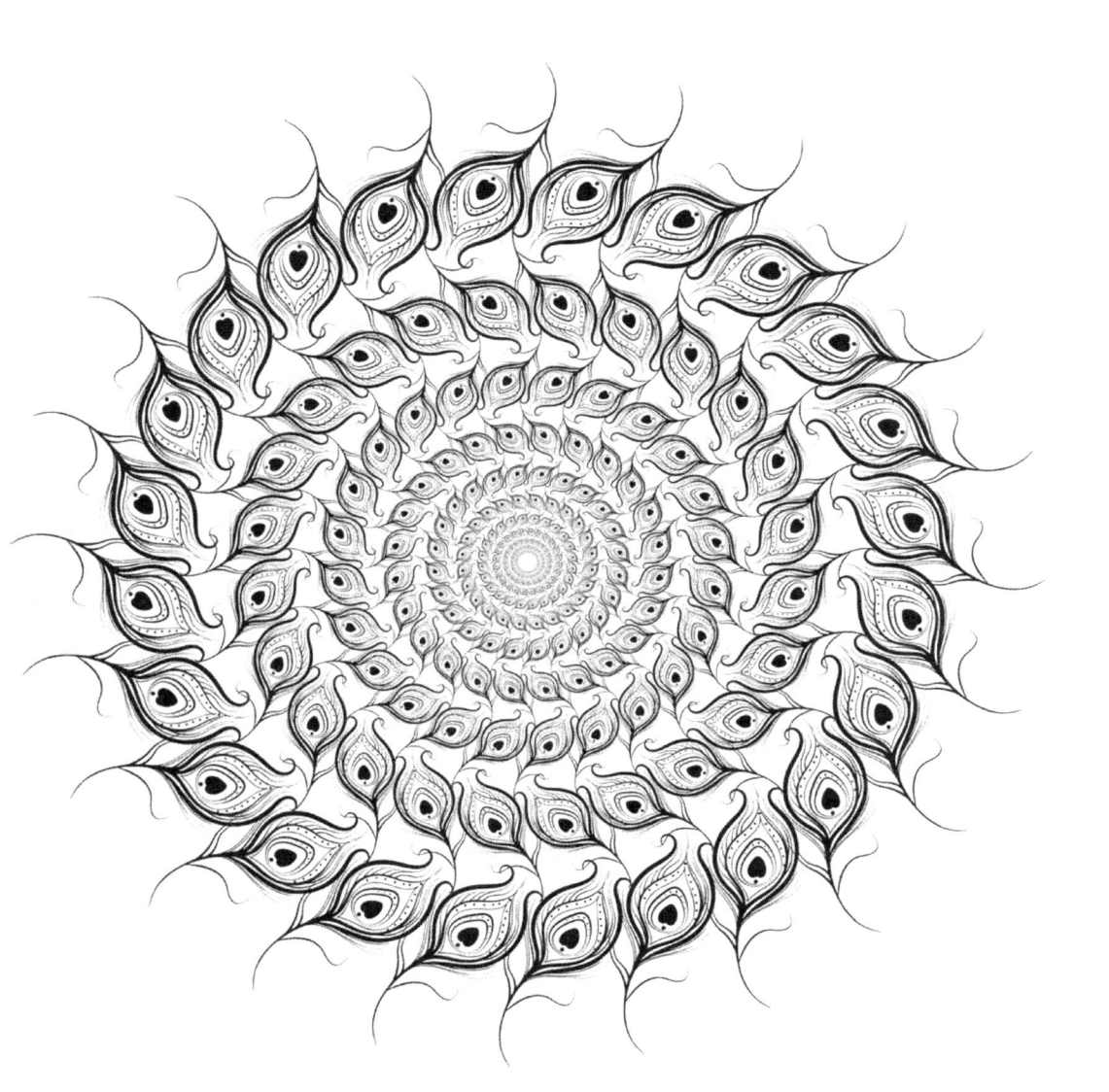

Where you focus, energy flows.

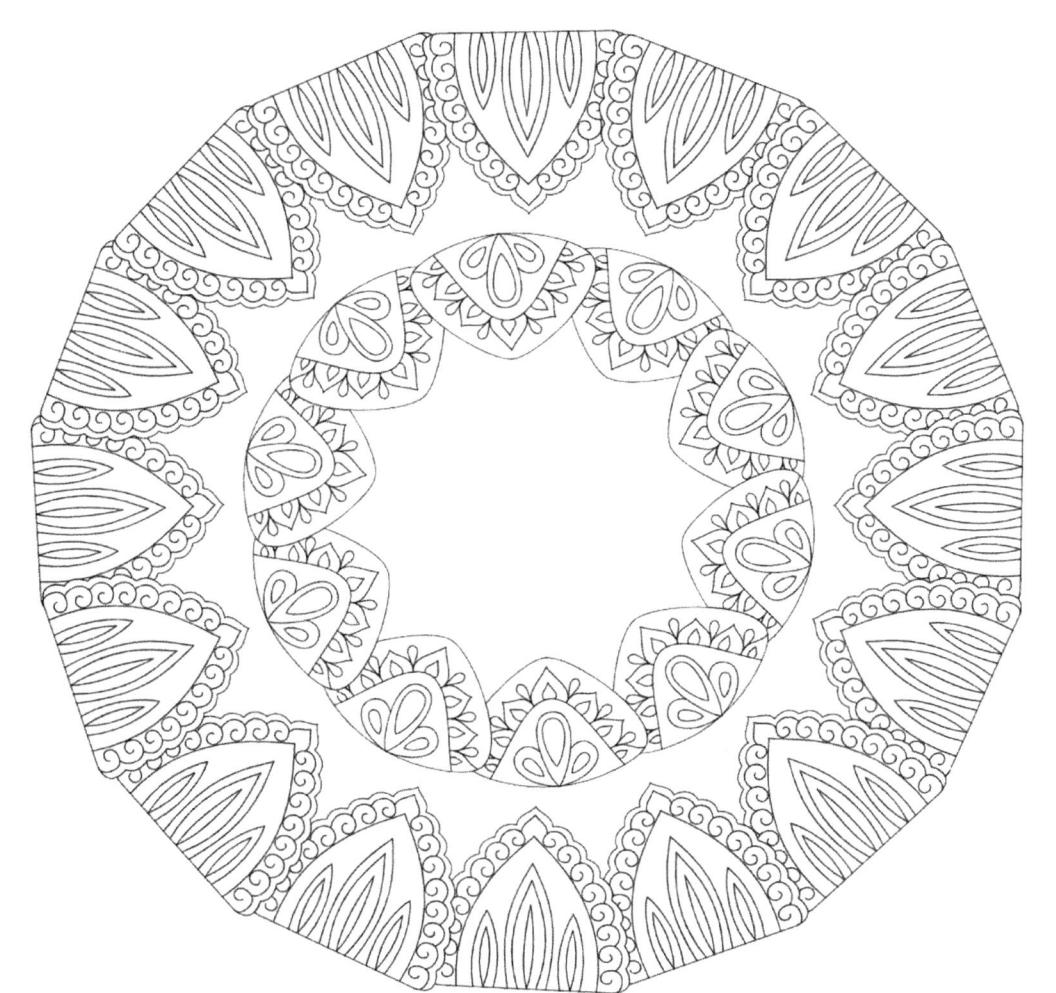

Disentangle.

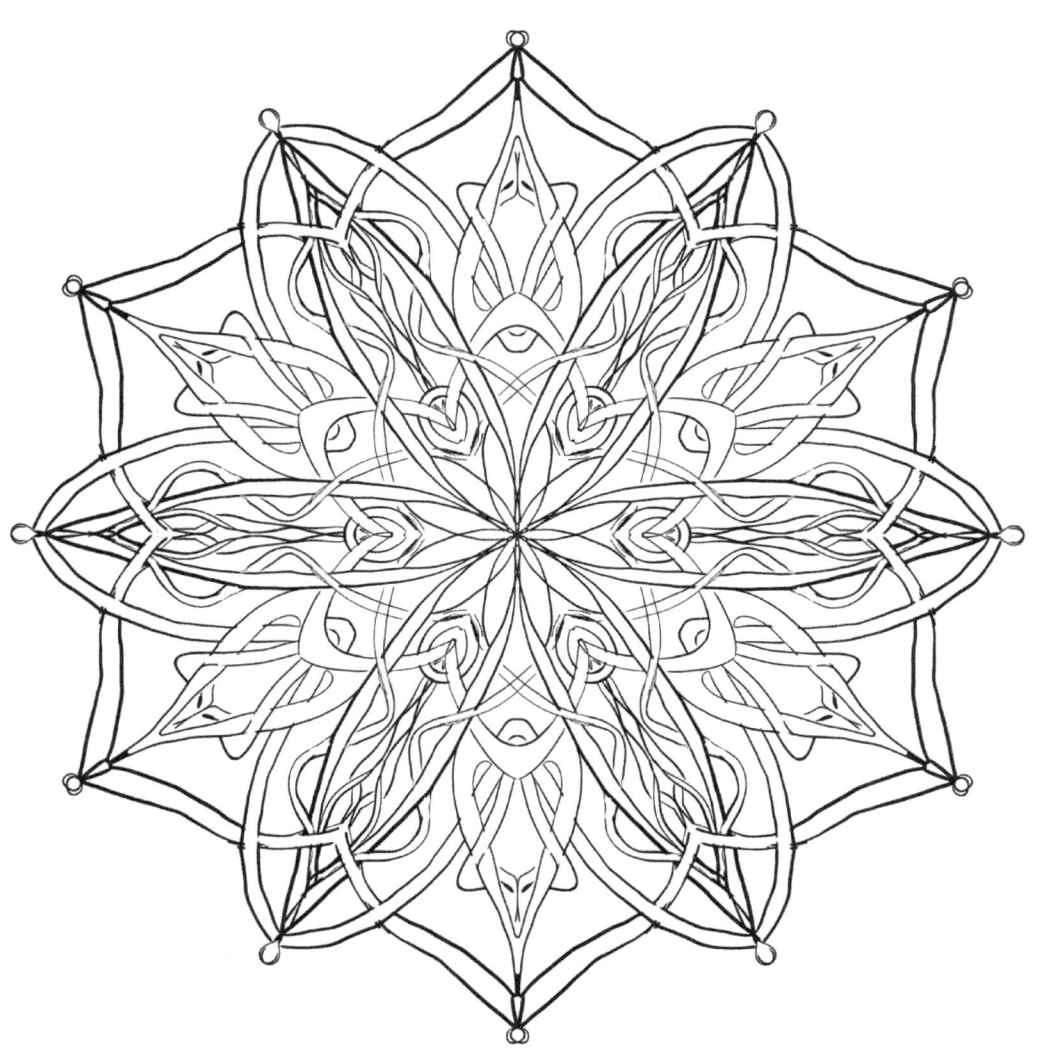

Stratify data, clear the mind.

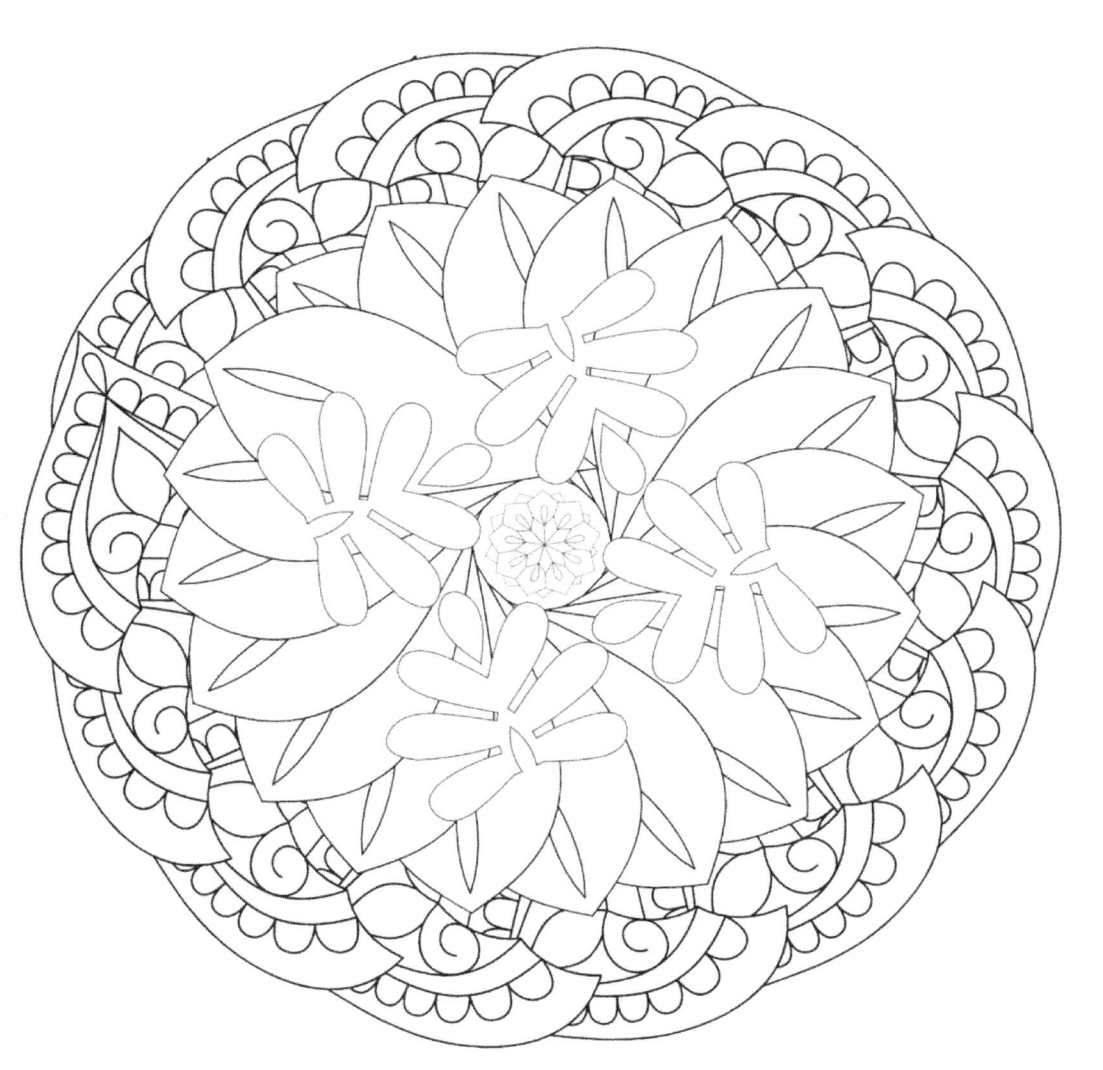

Untangle the nets.

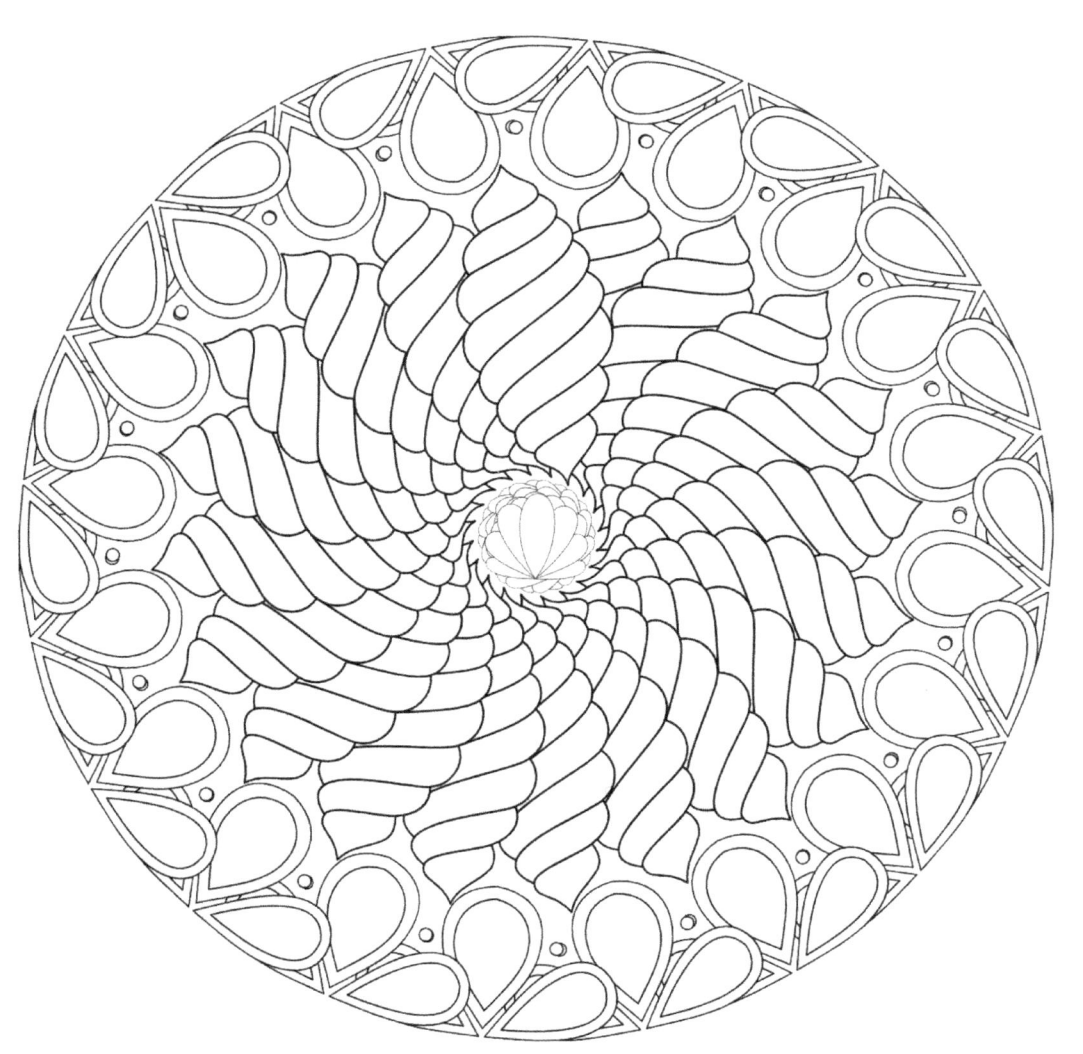

Sometime you just need to stop and contemplate.

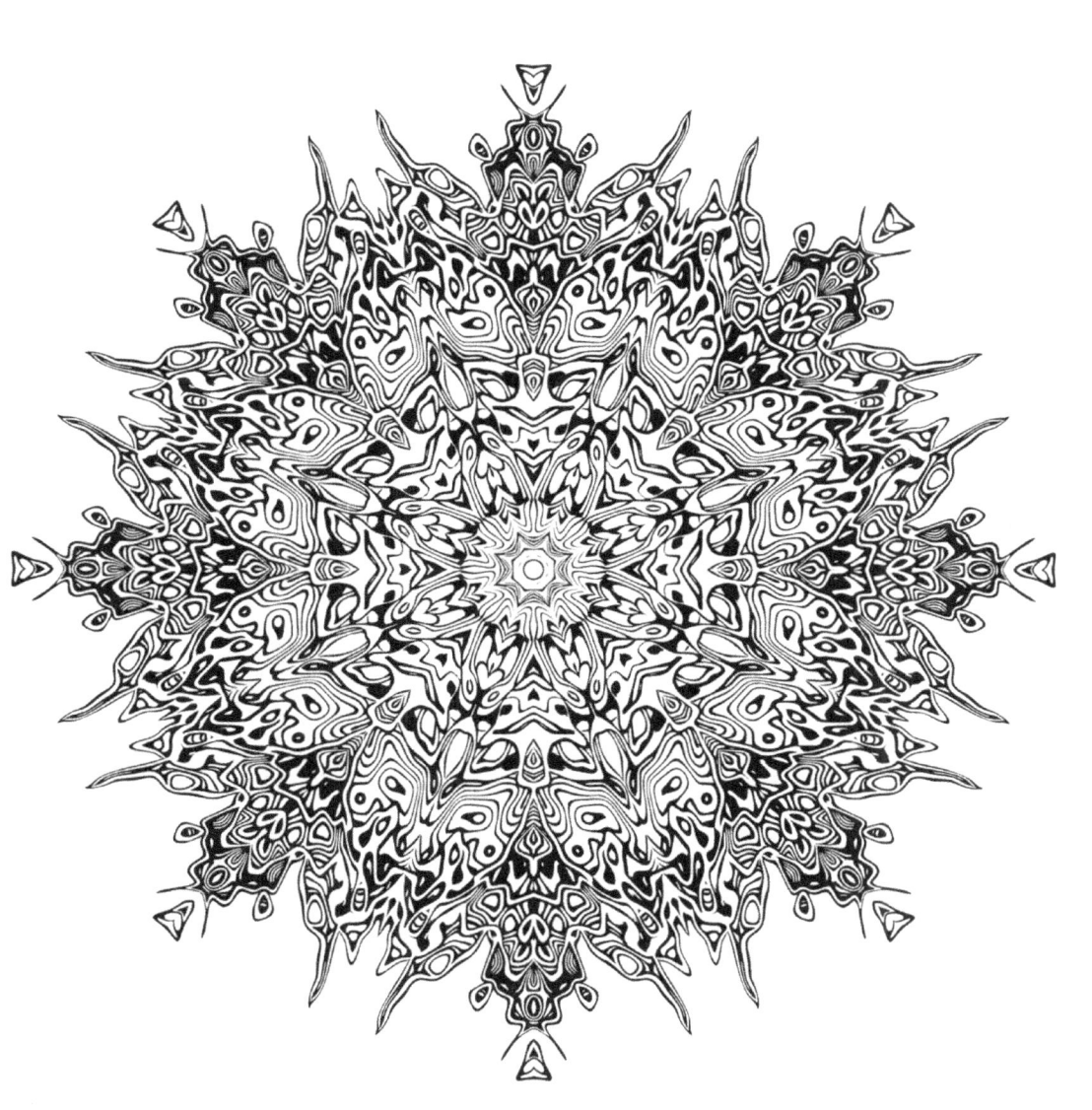

Divide into important parts.

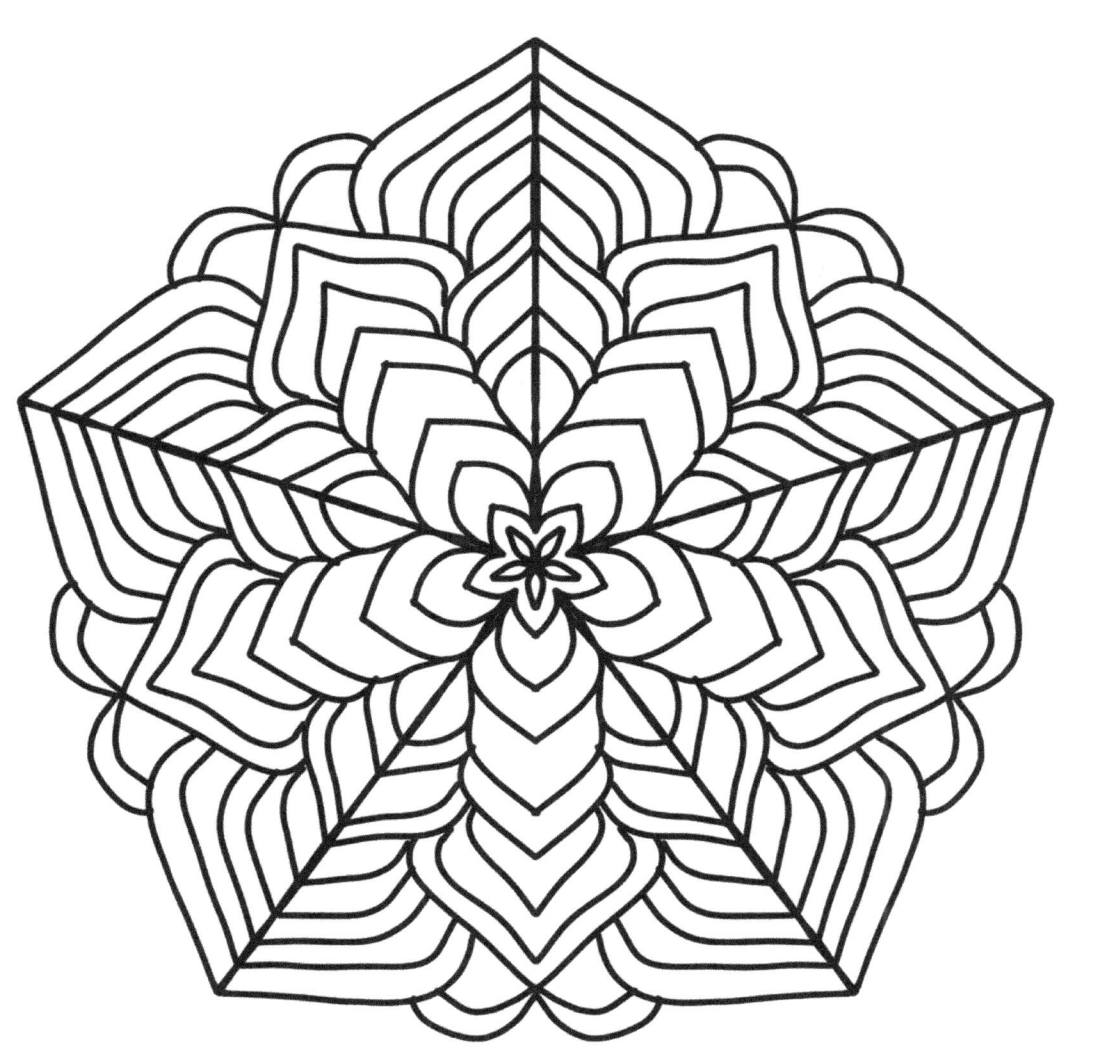

Your culture is not the only one.

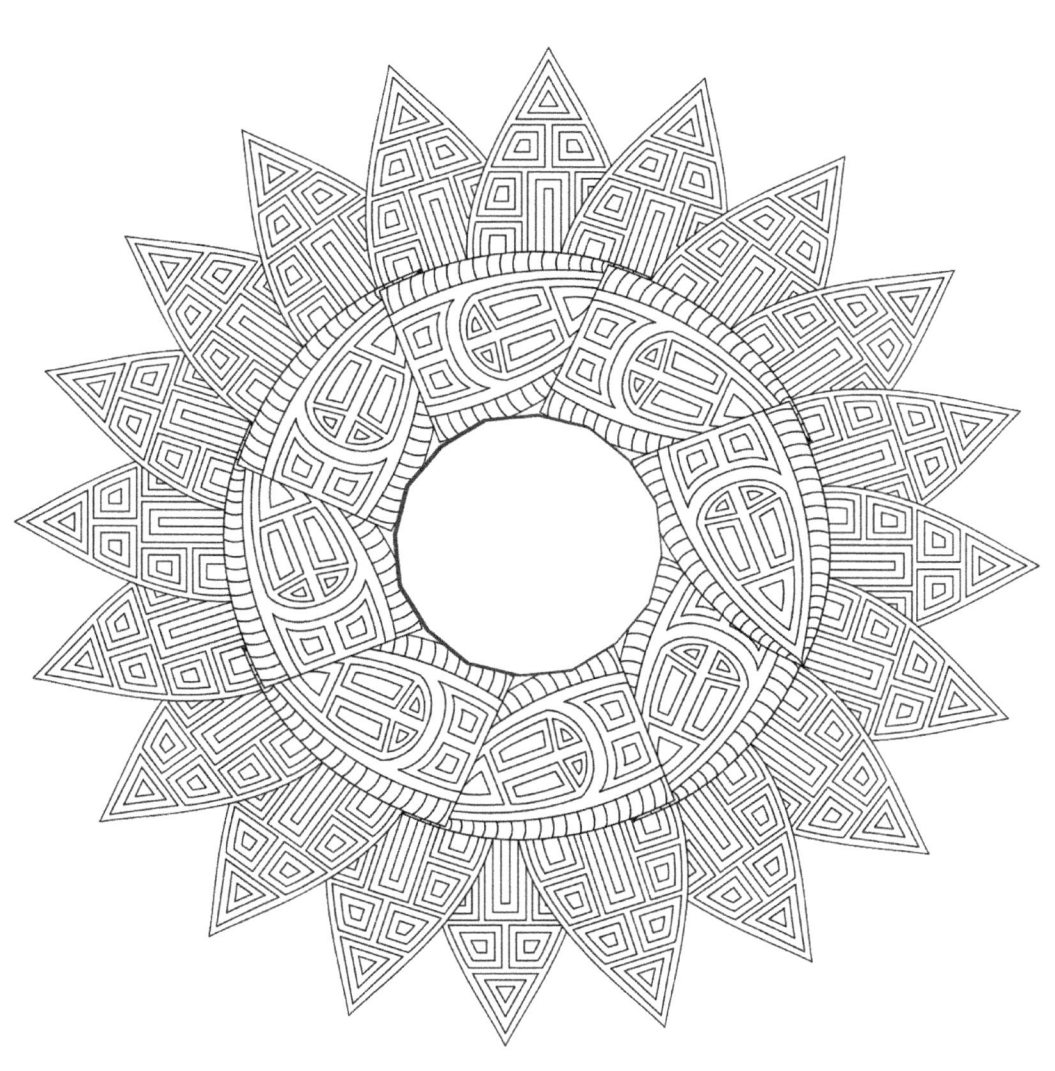

Expand the borders.

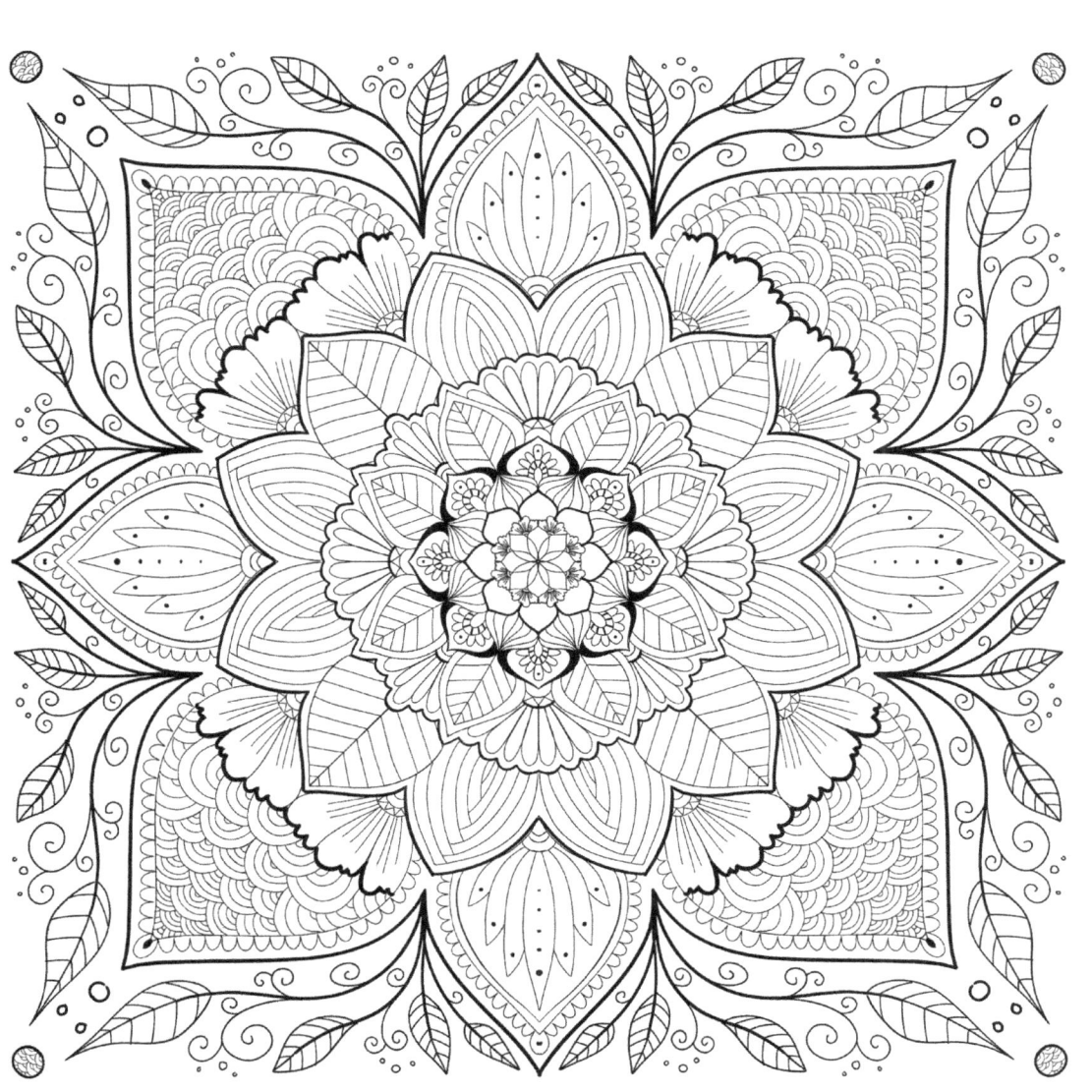

Do you feel something is wrong?
Fix it.

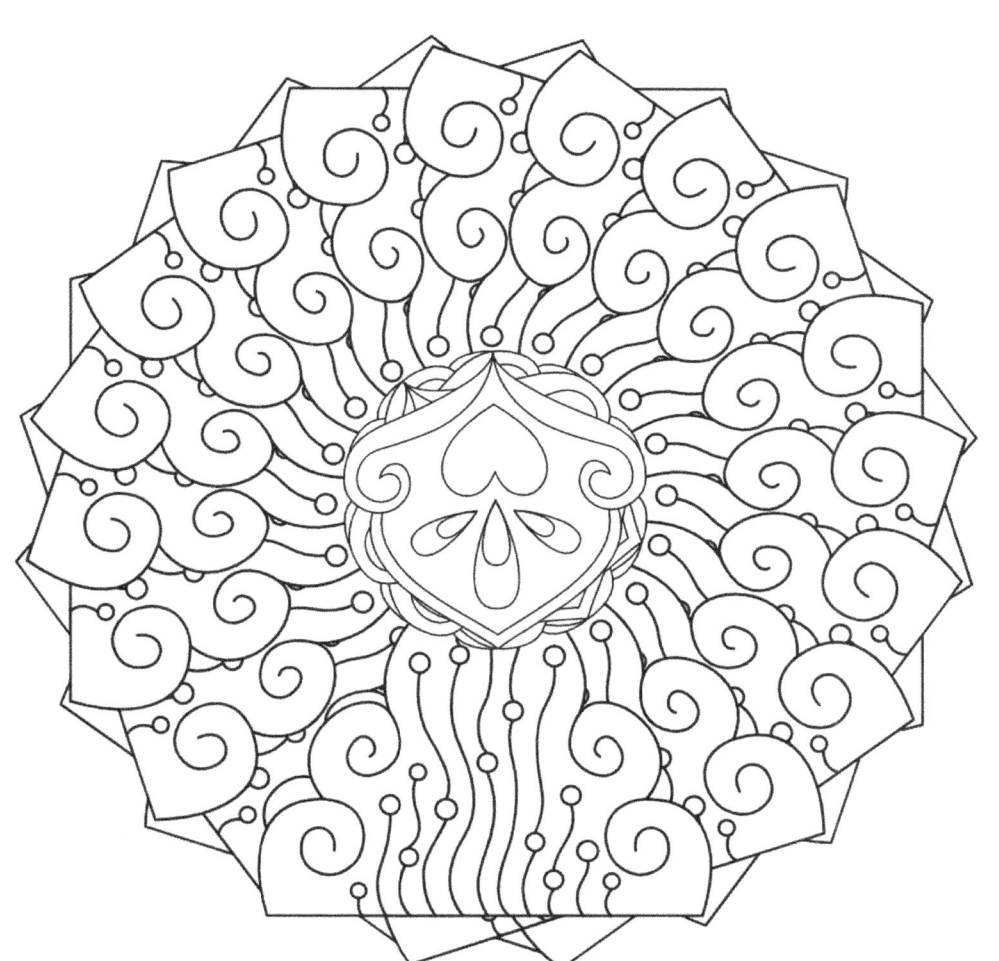

Defend your rights.

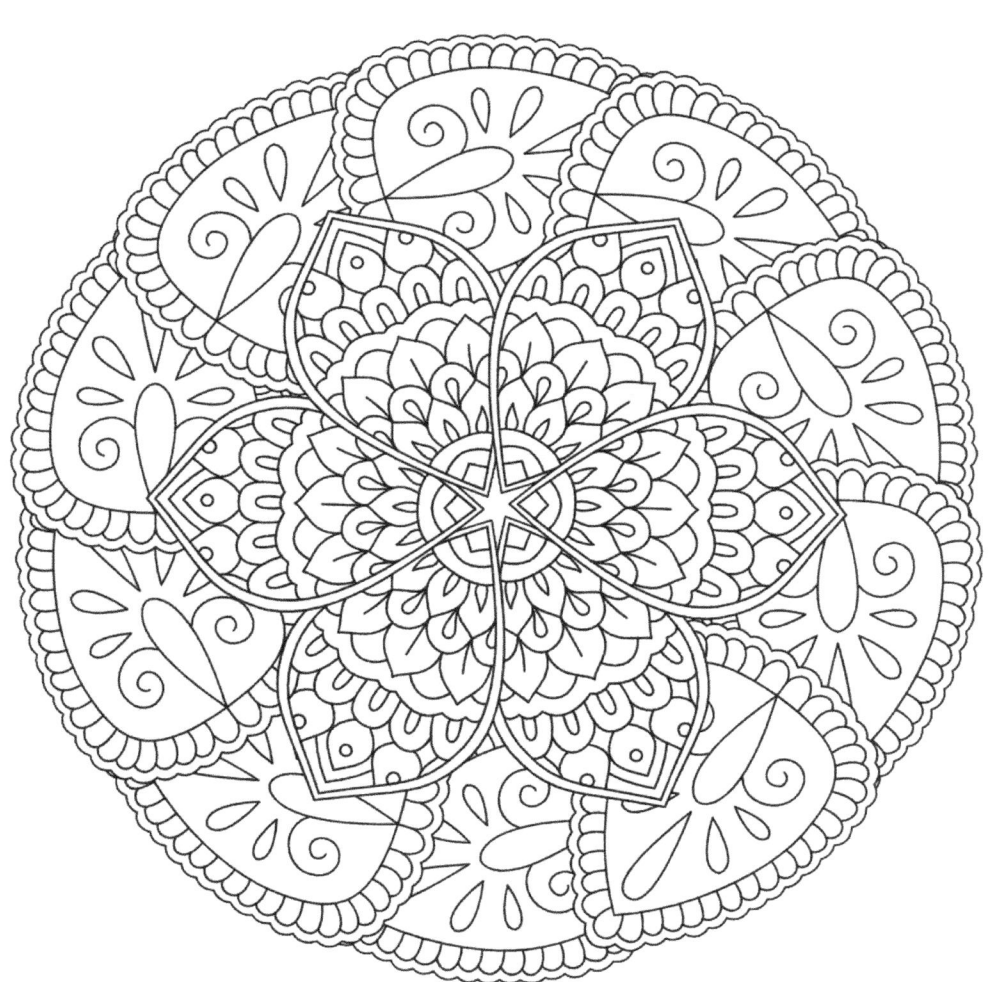

The sun never quits shining.

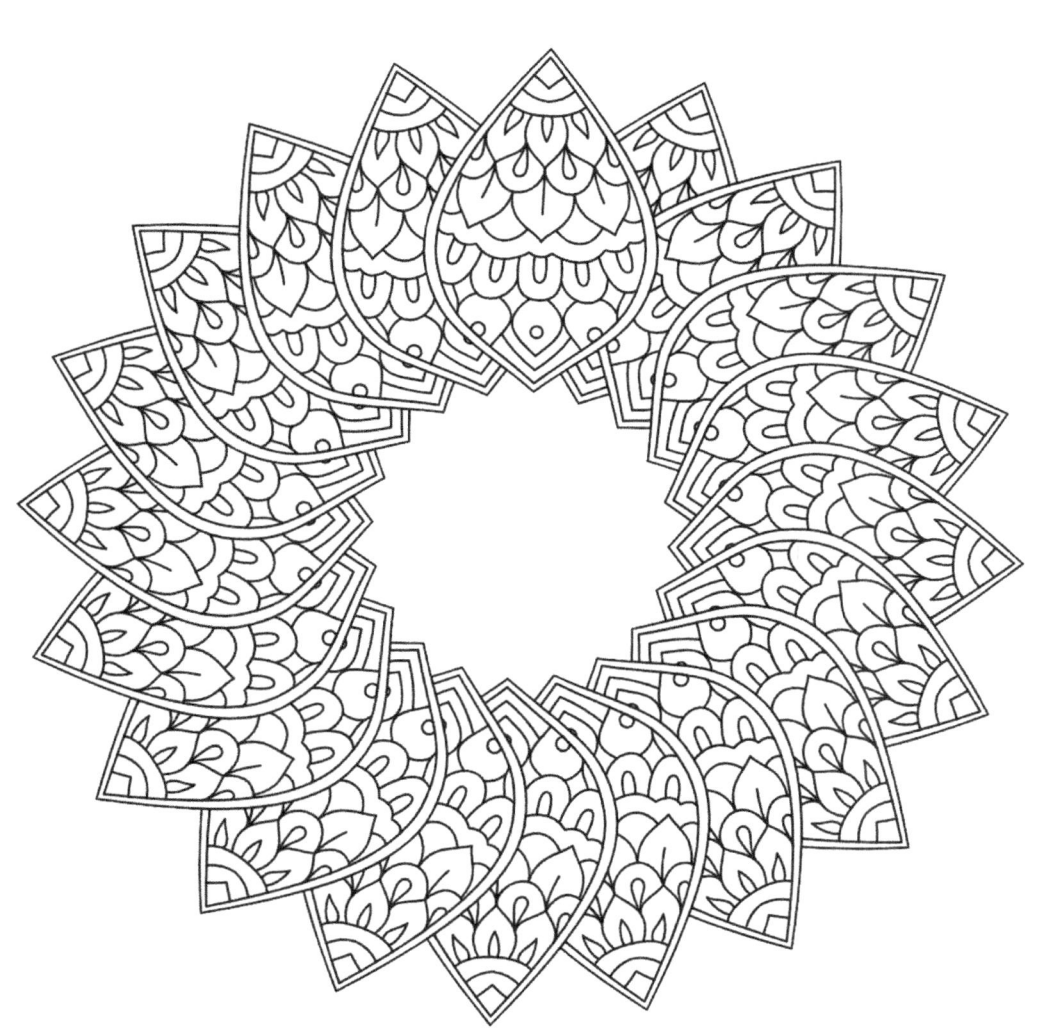

It all comes from the inside.

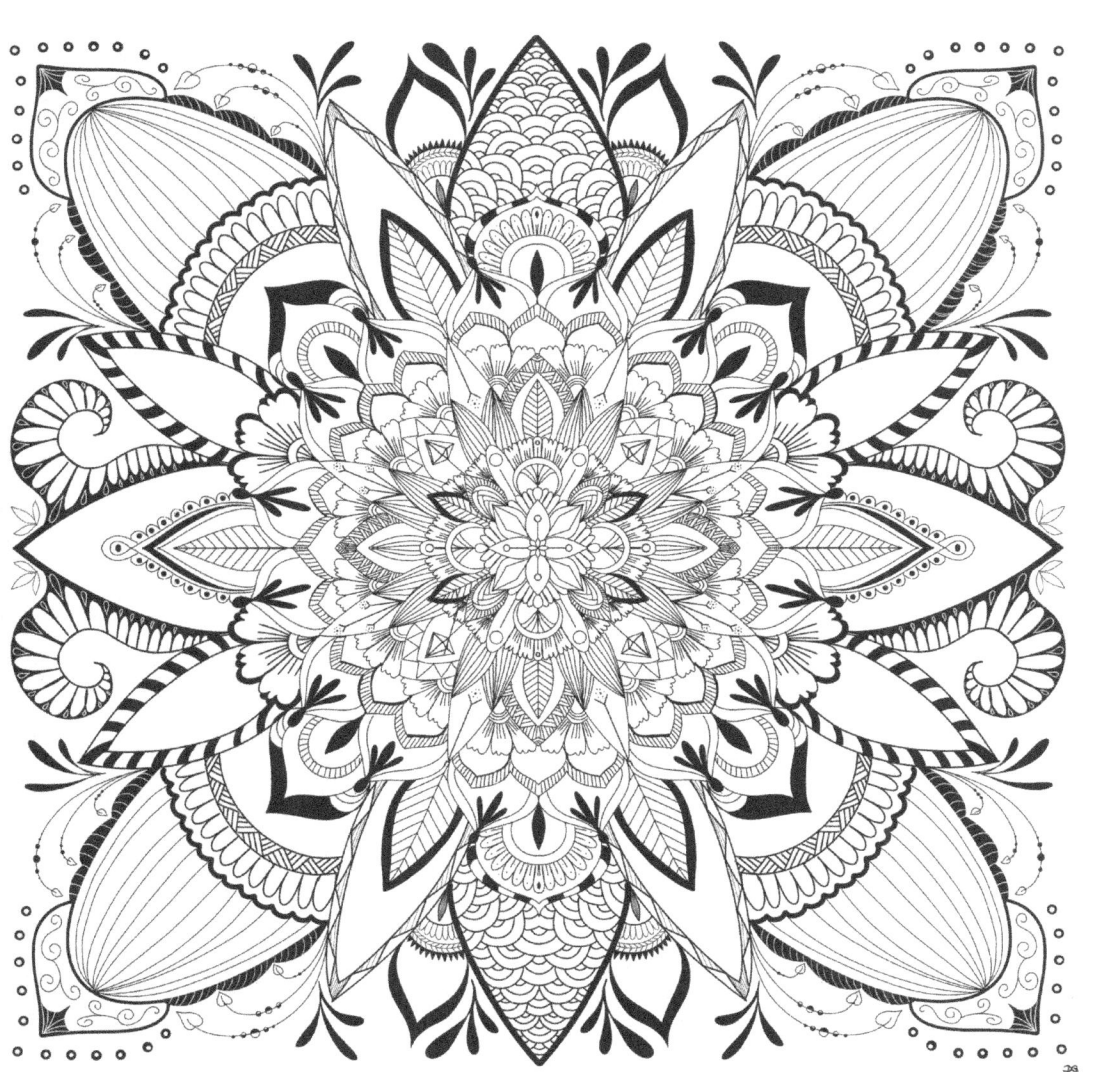

Feel comfortable to go from complexity...

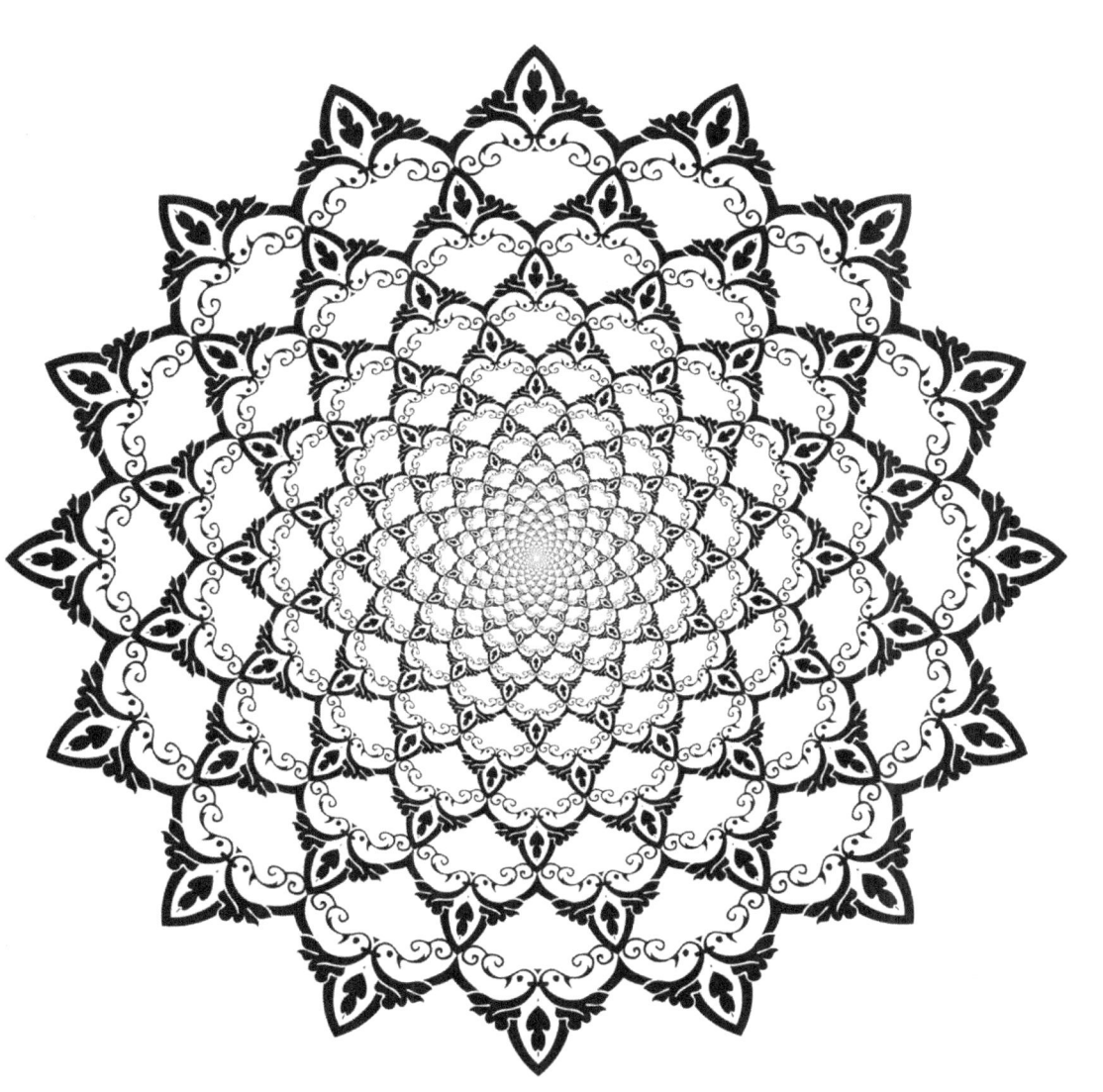

. . . to simplicity.

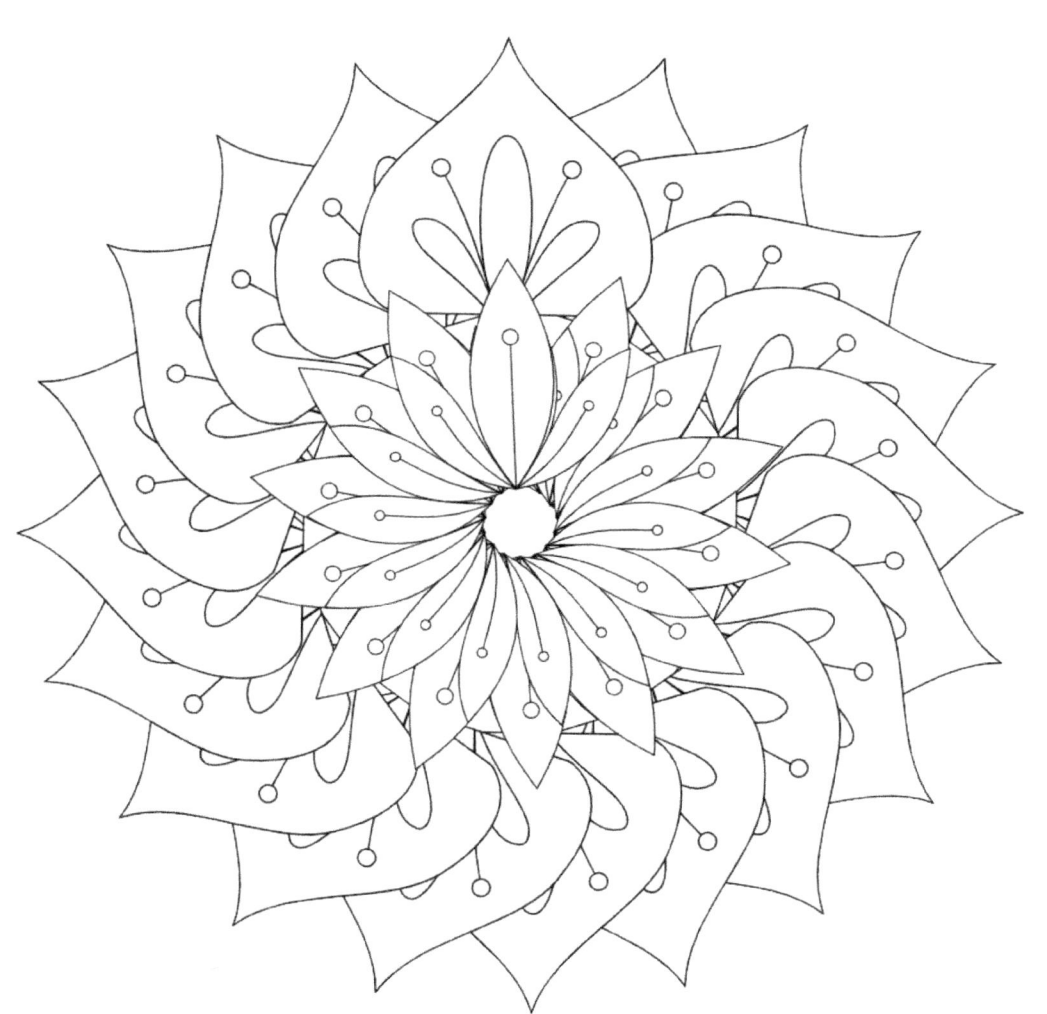

Just have fun.

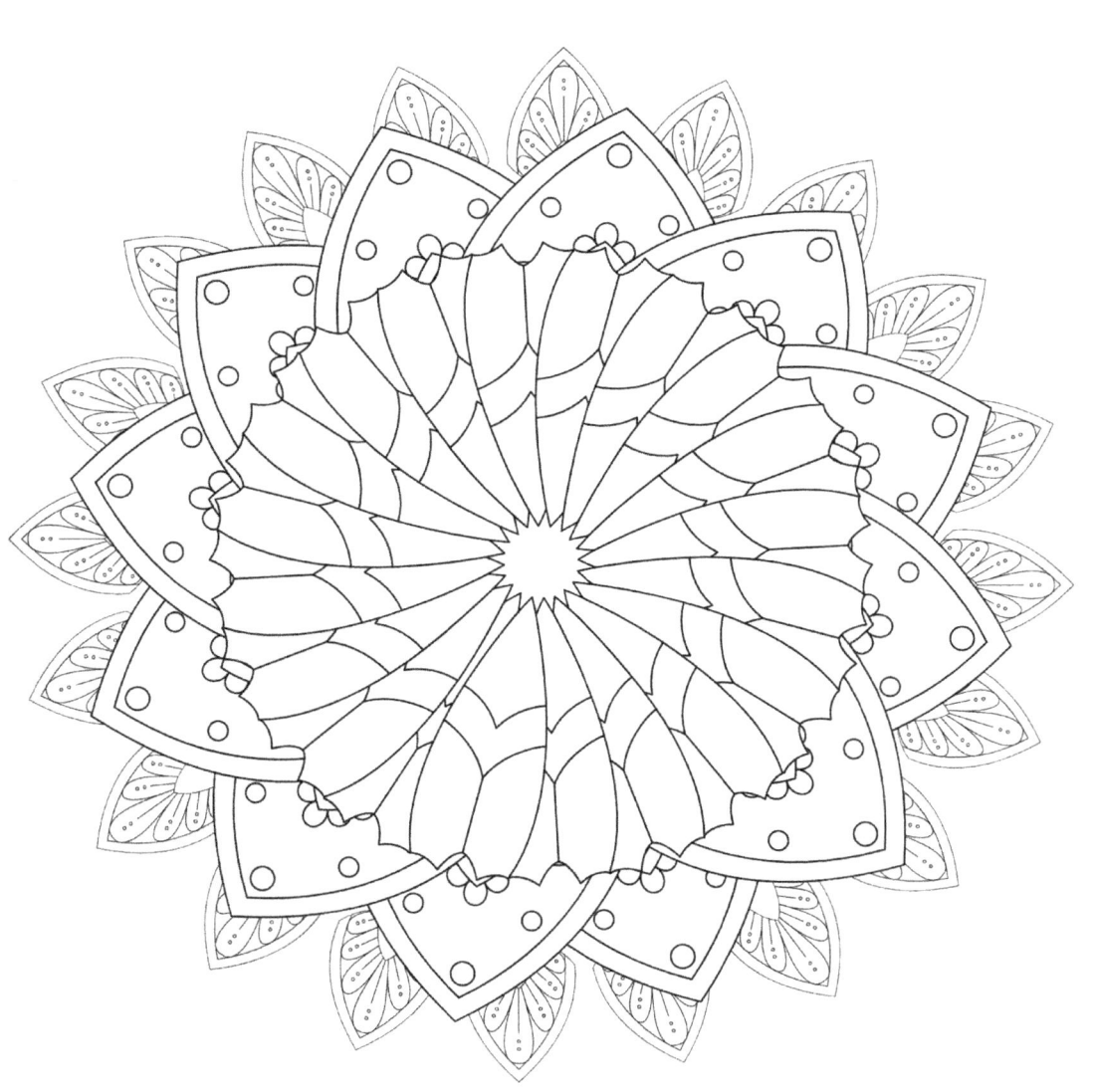

What does it come to your mind?

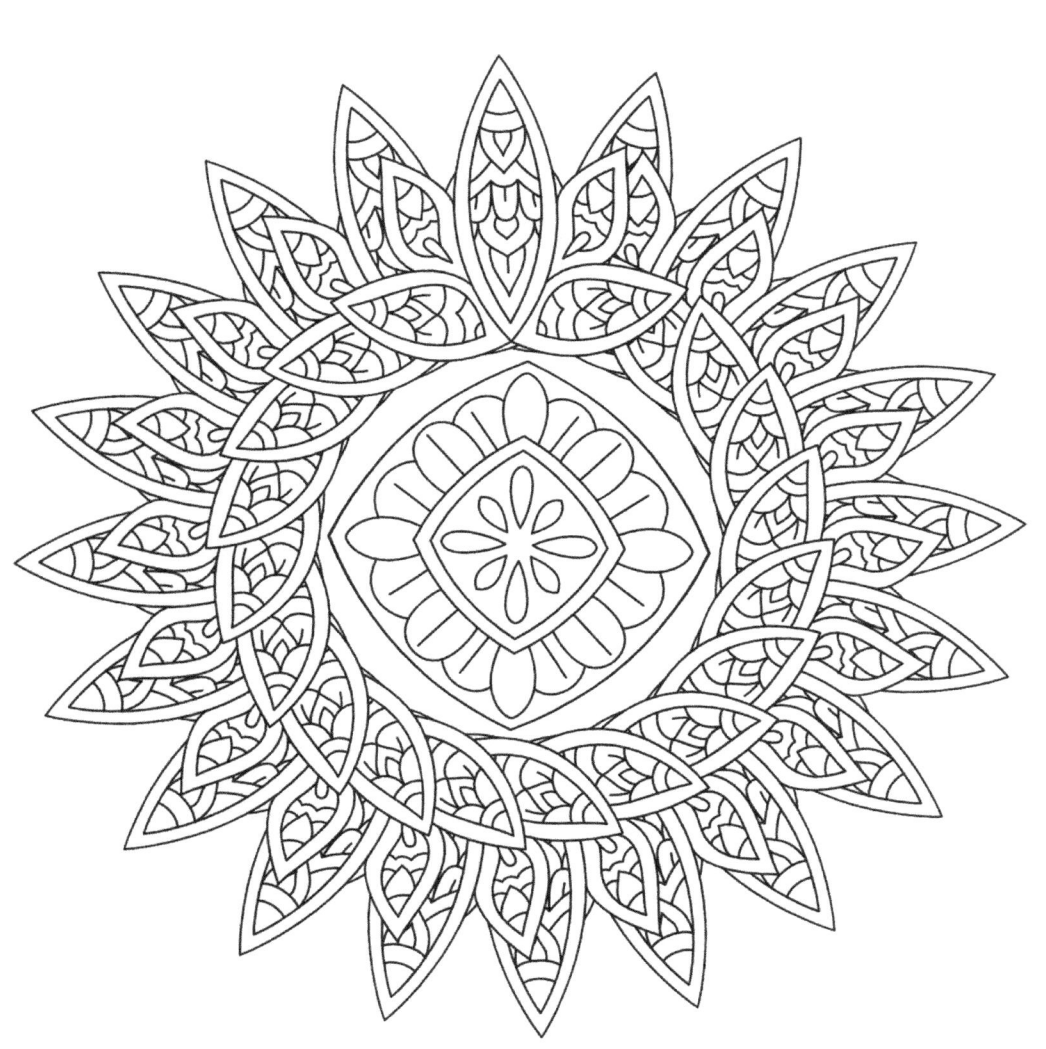

Ring at the door.

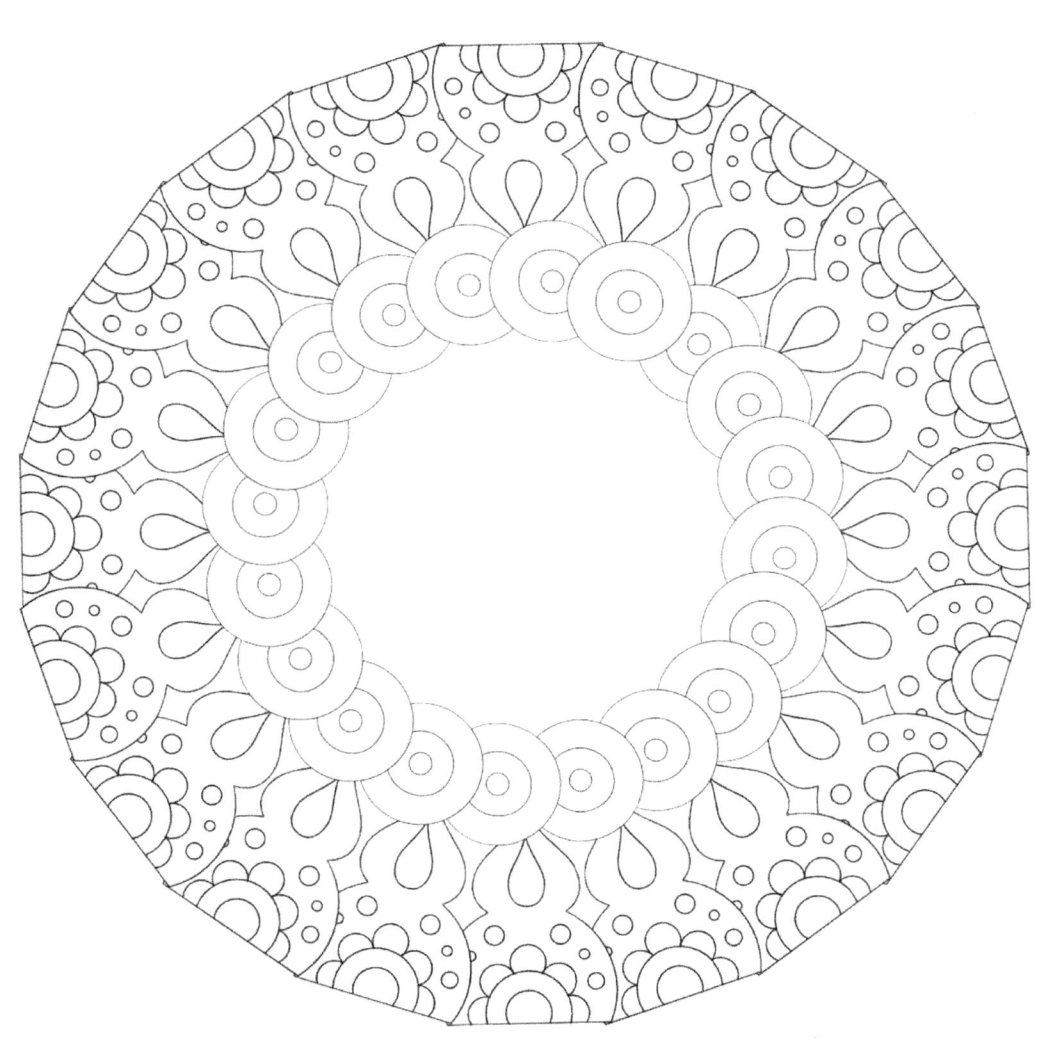

Other times you should feel comfortable to go from simplicity...

. . .to complexity.

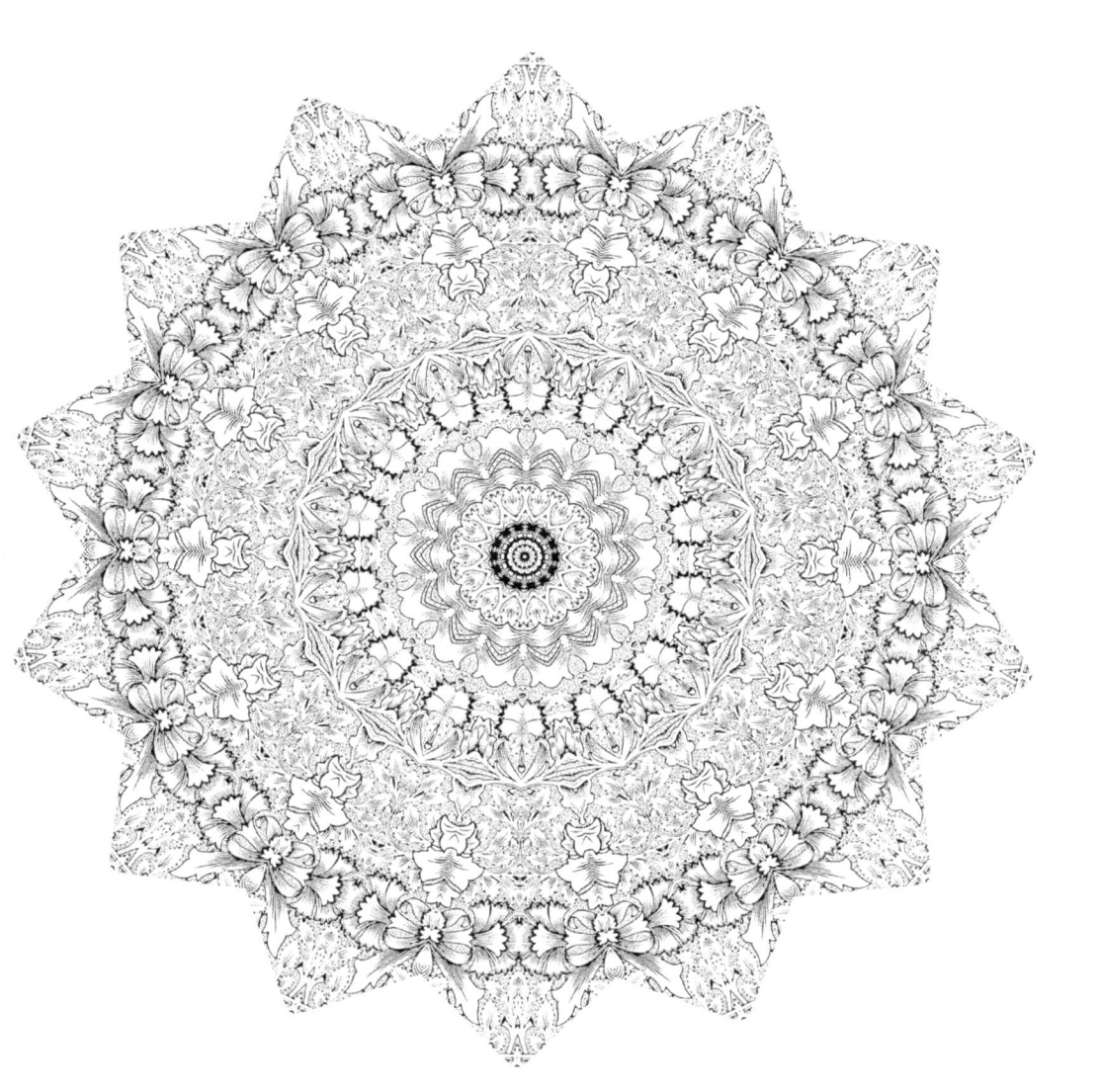

Try half, if good duplicate it.

Embrace strangeness...

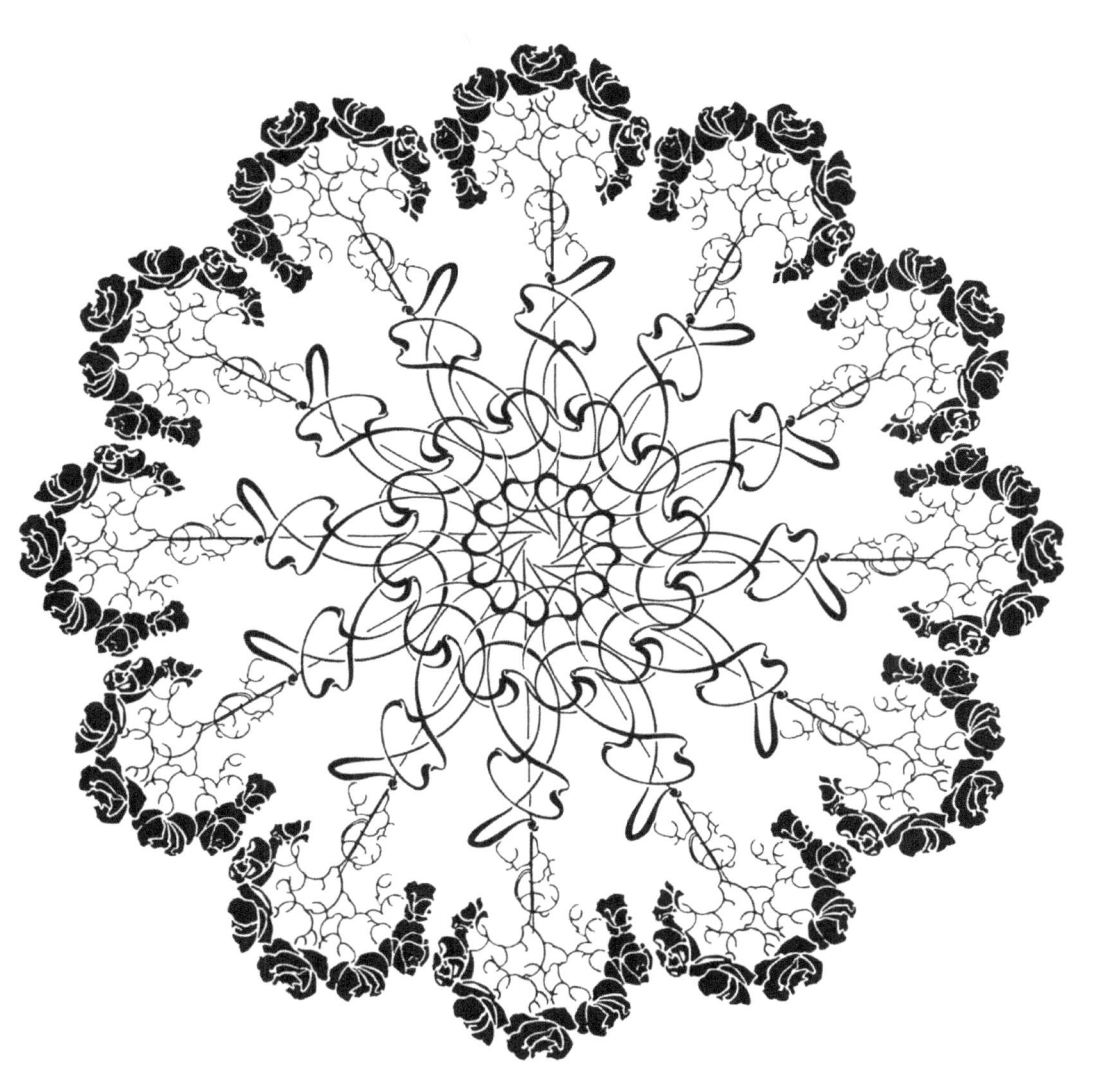

. . . whatever its form.

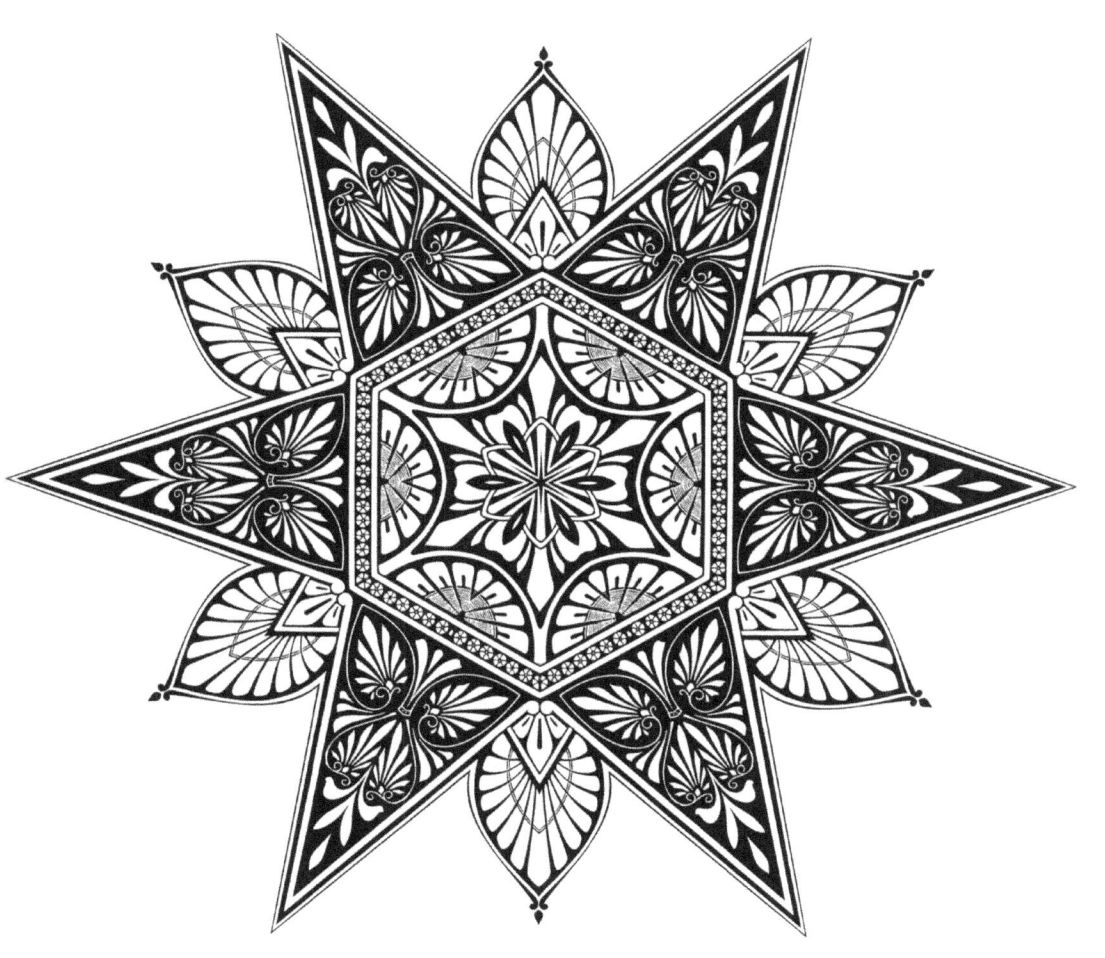

Drop by drop.

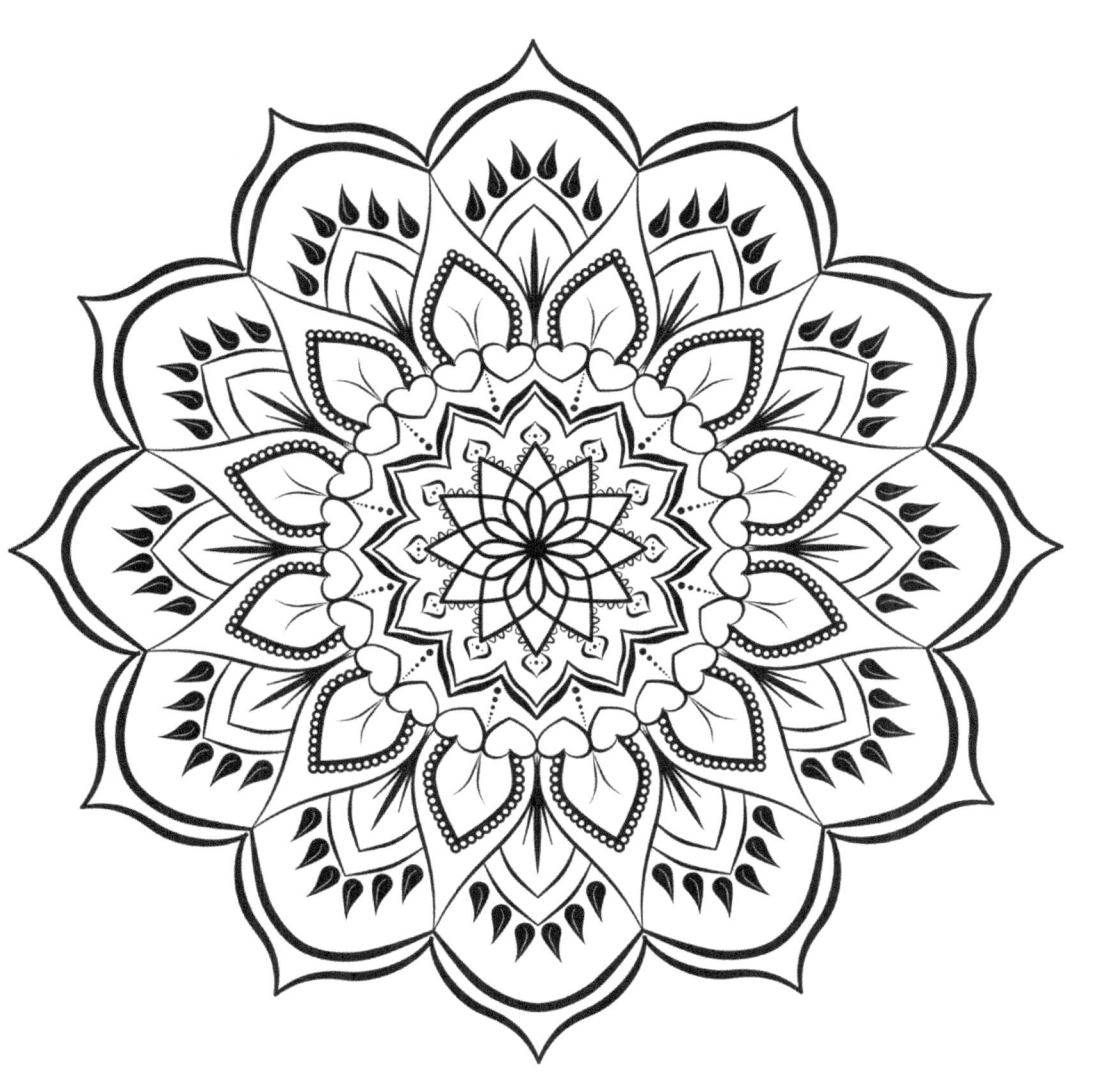

Find your circus.

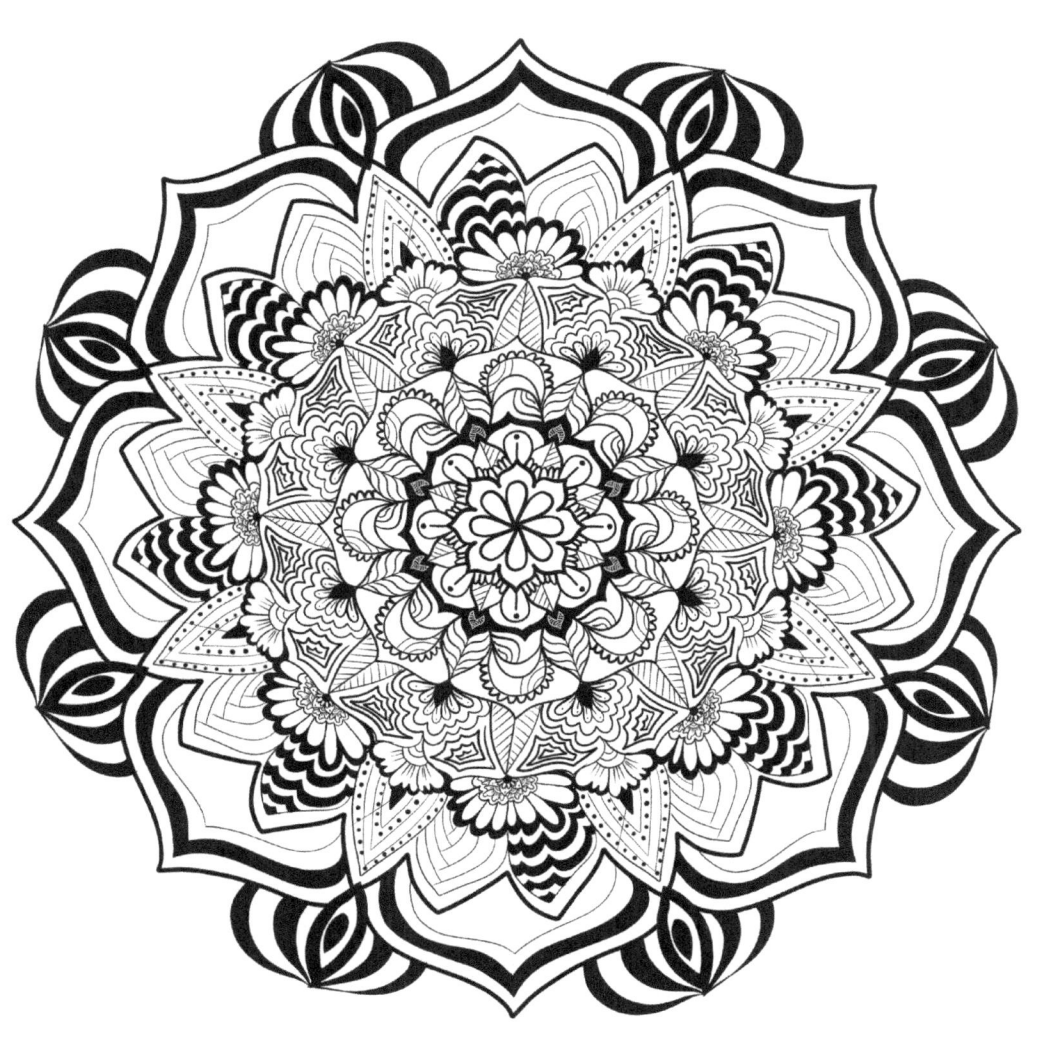

Connect the dots.

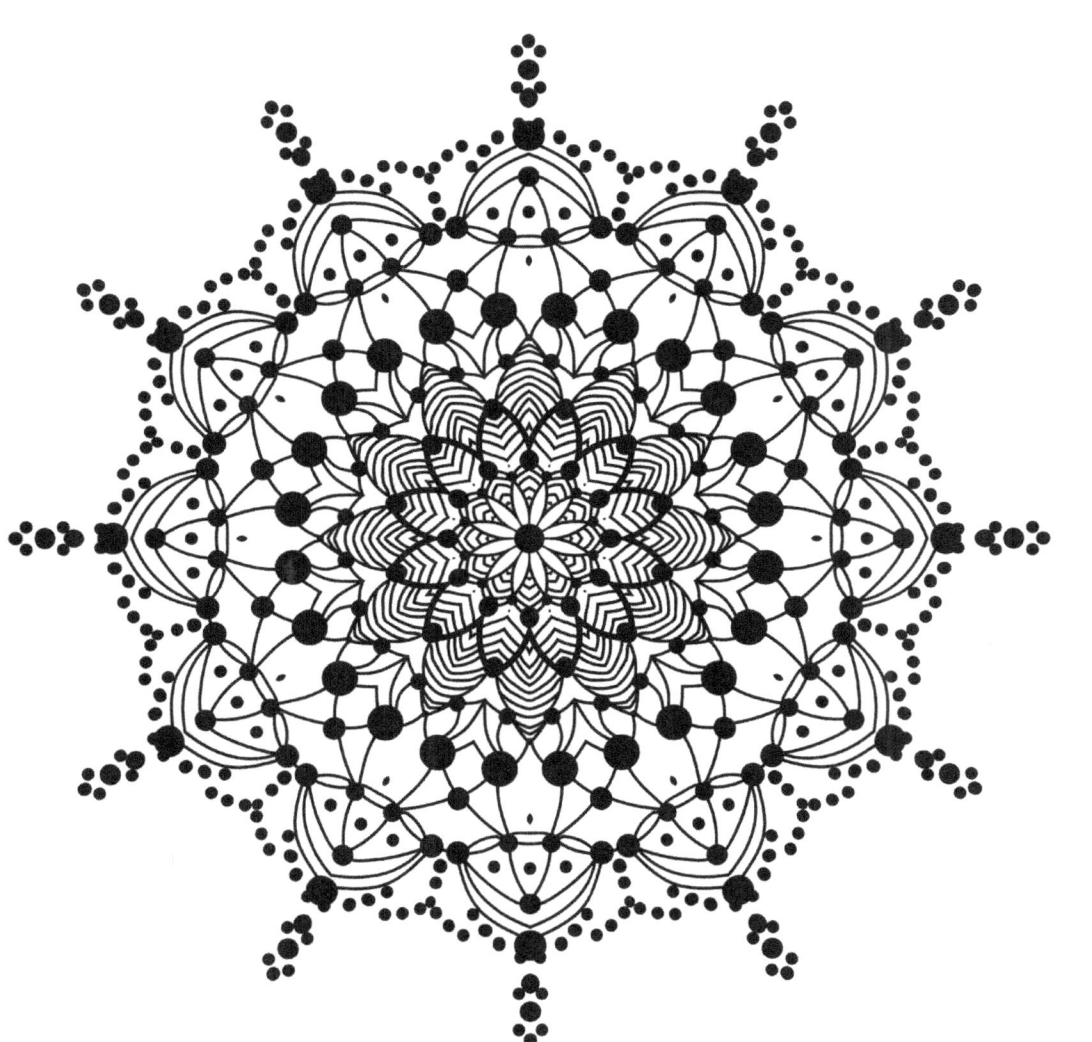

*Good, bad, who knows?
Learn to reframe life events.*

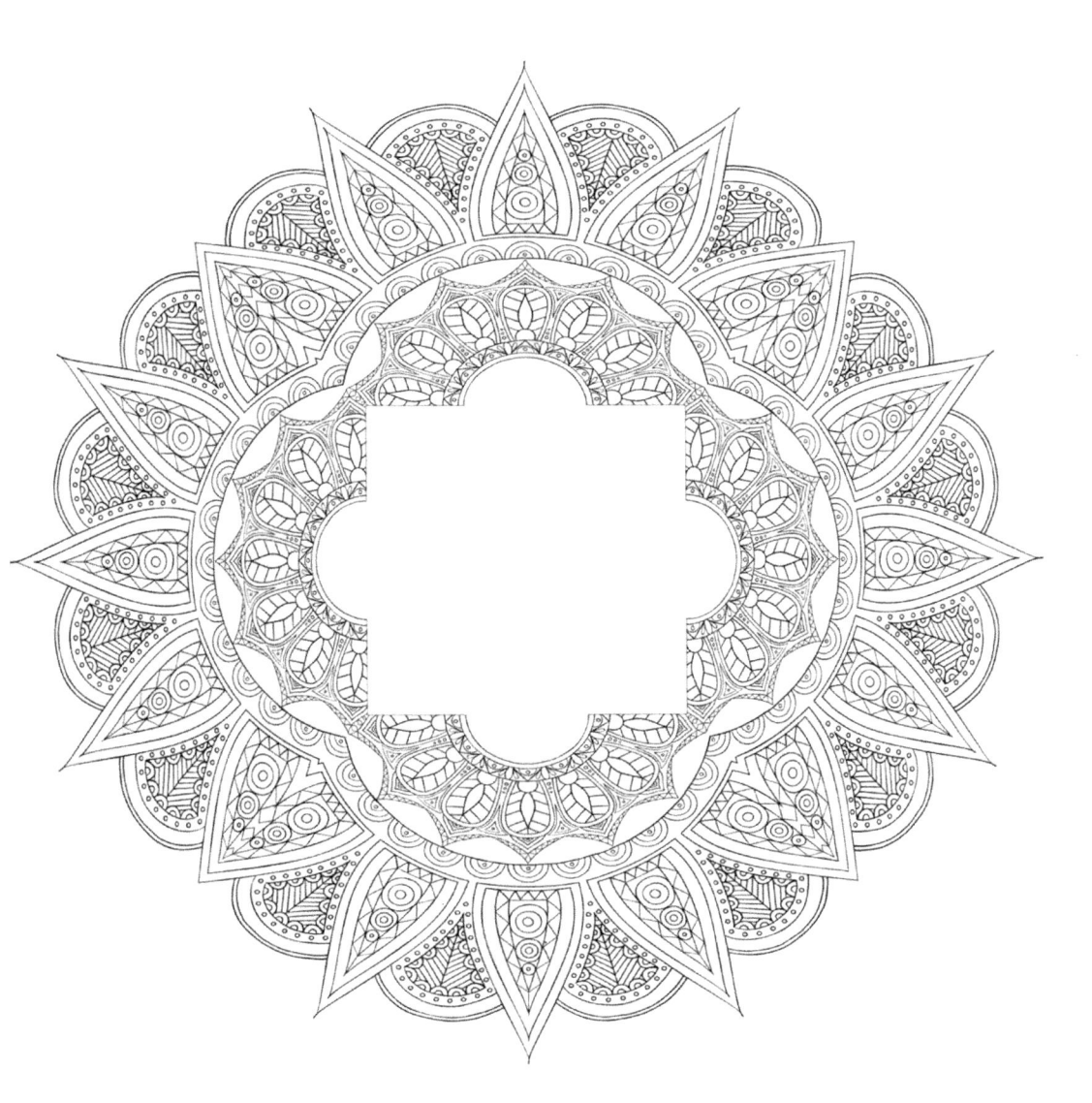

Make plans and rely on them.

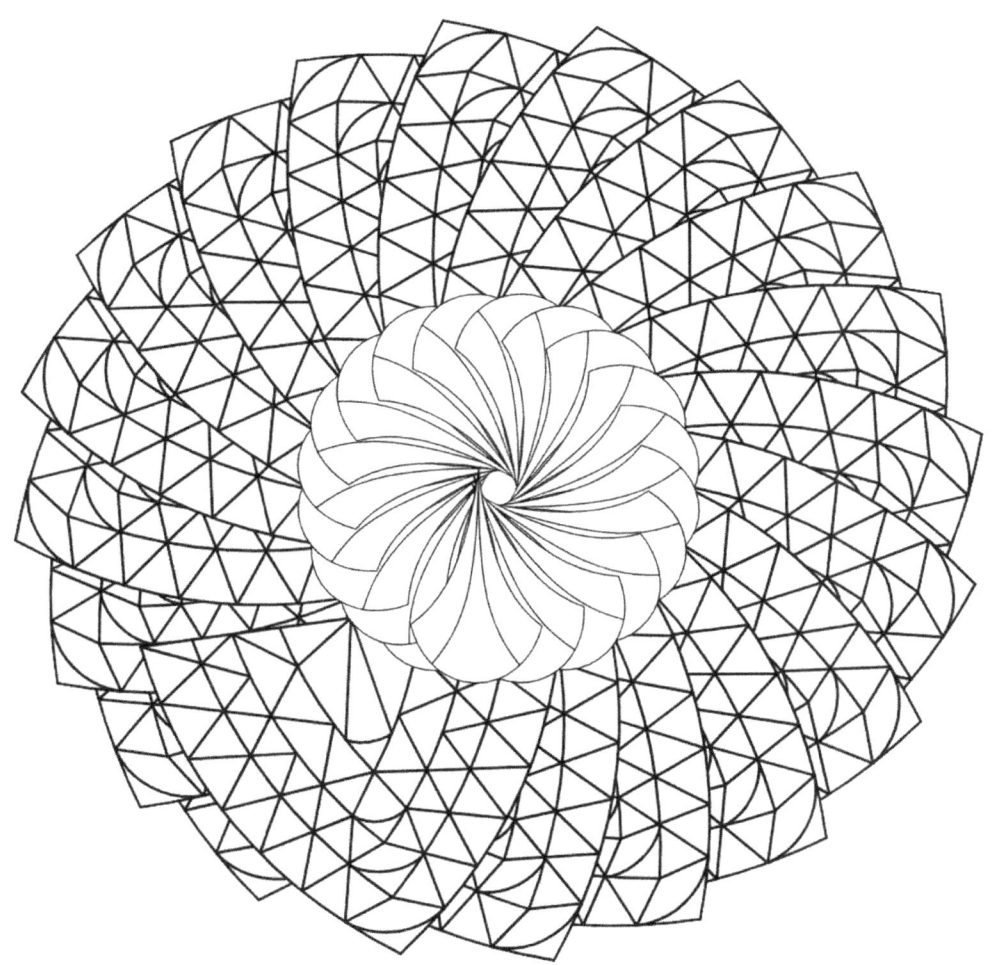

You can find more needles than you expect.

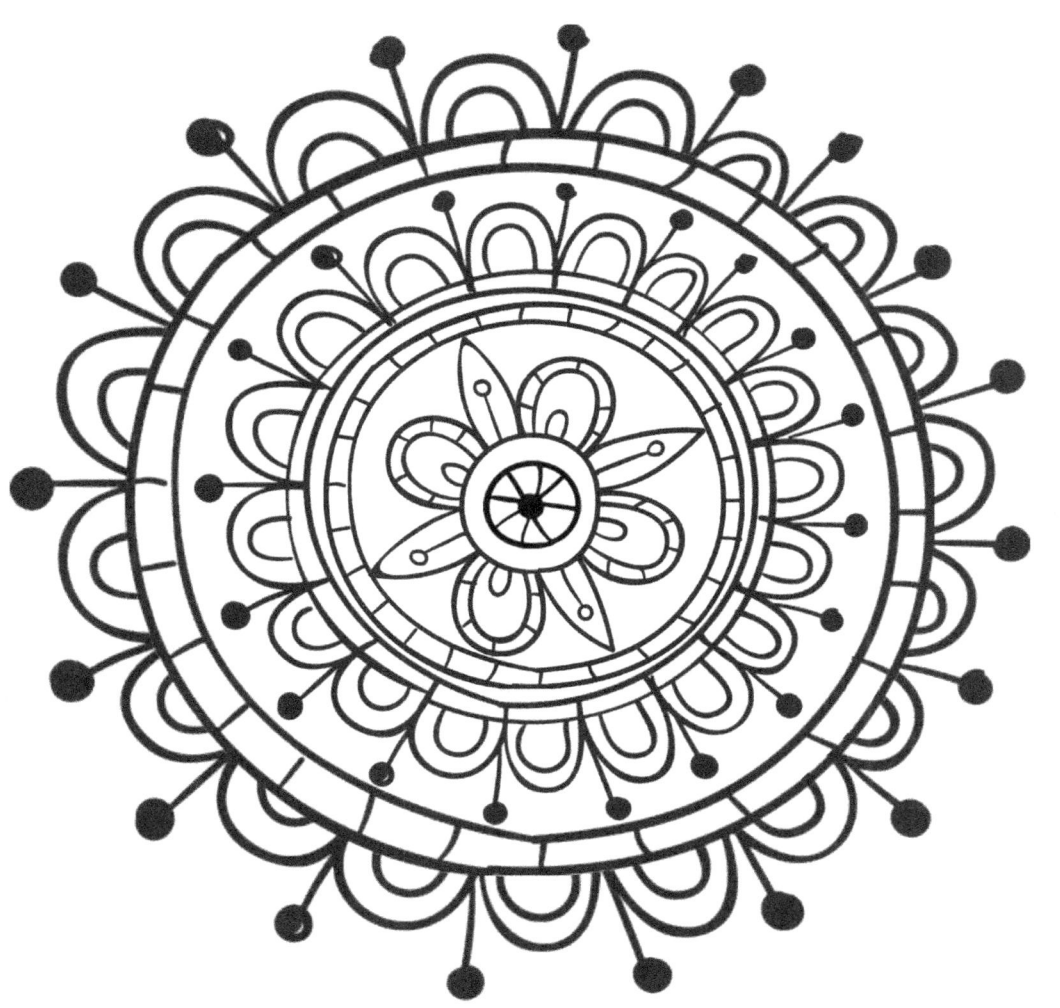

Face the dark, see the light.

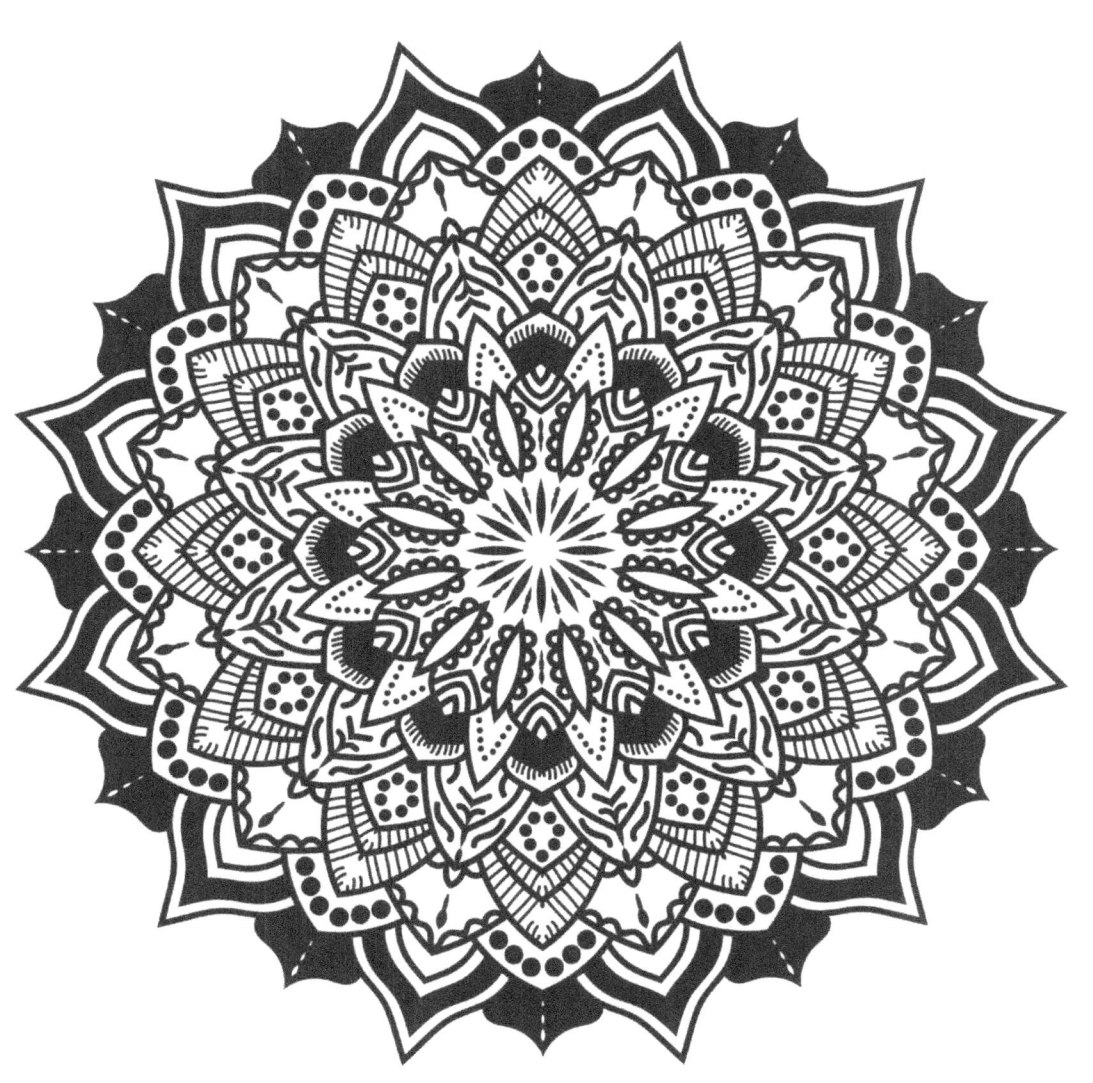

Savour to the full.

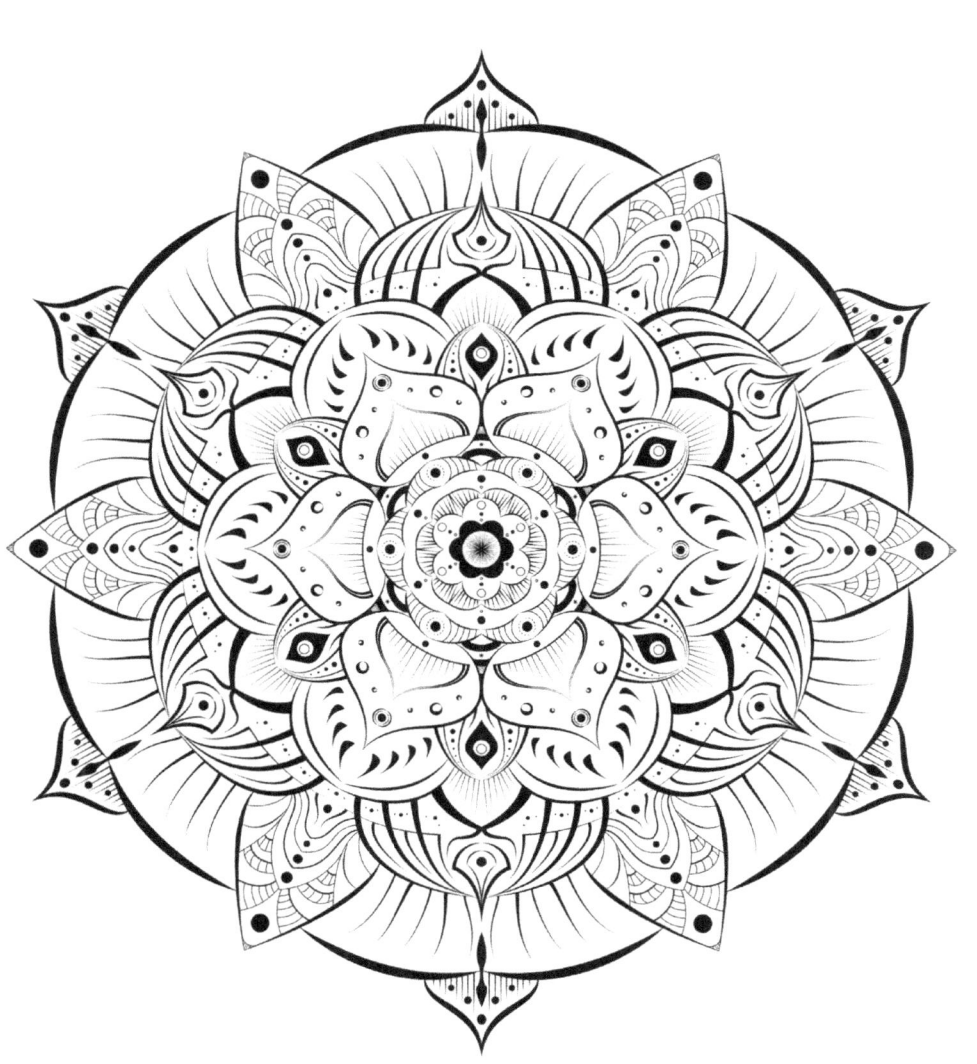

Endless peace.

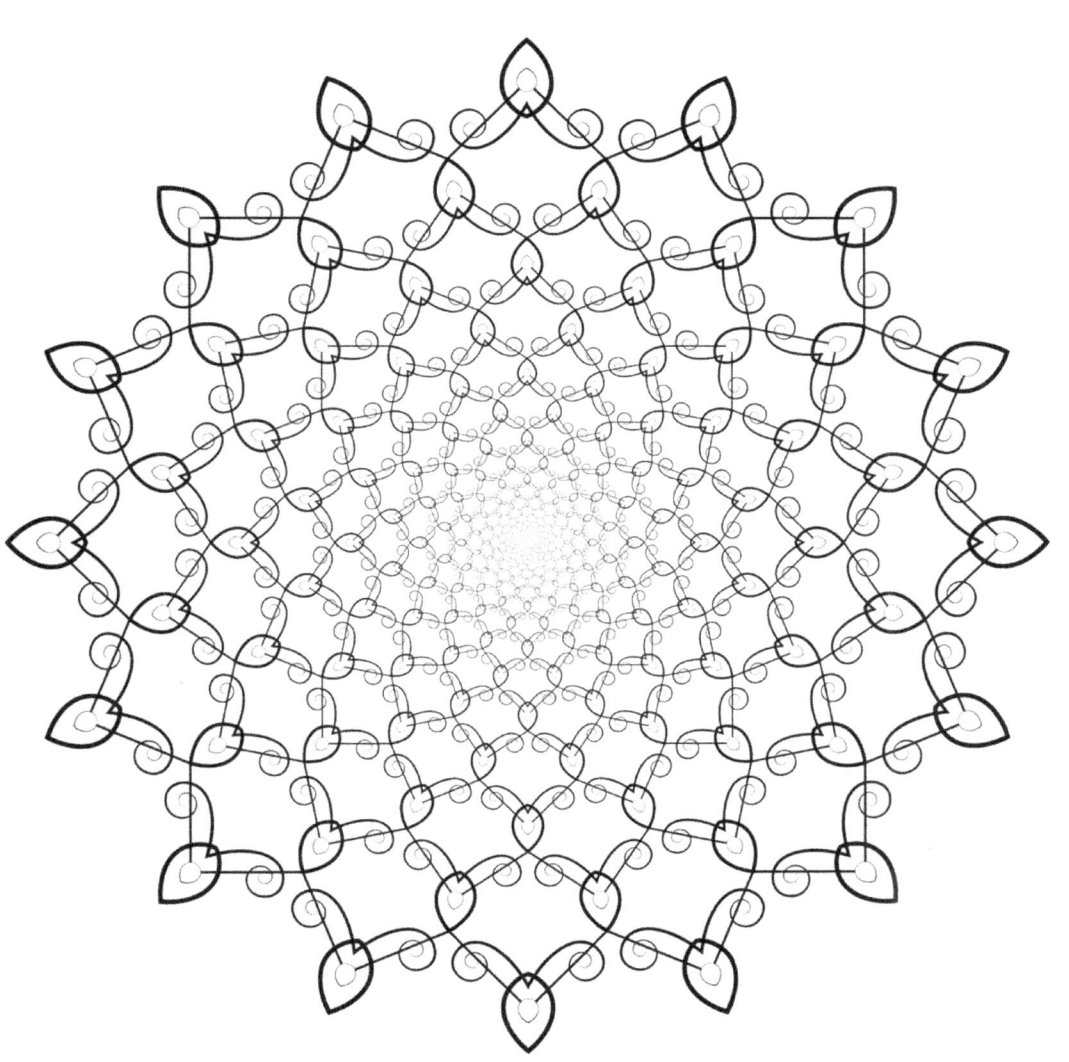

Enjoy your senses.

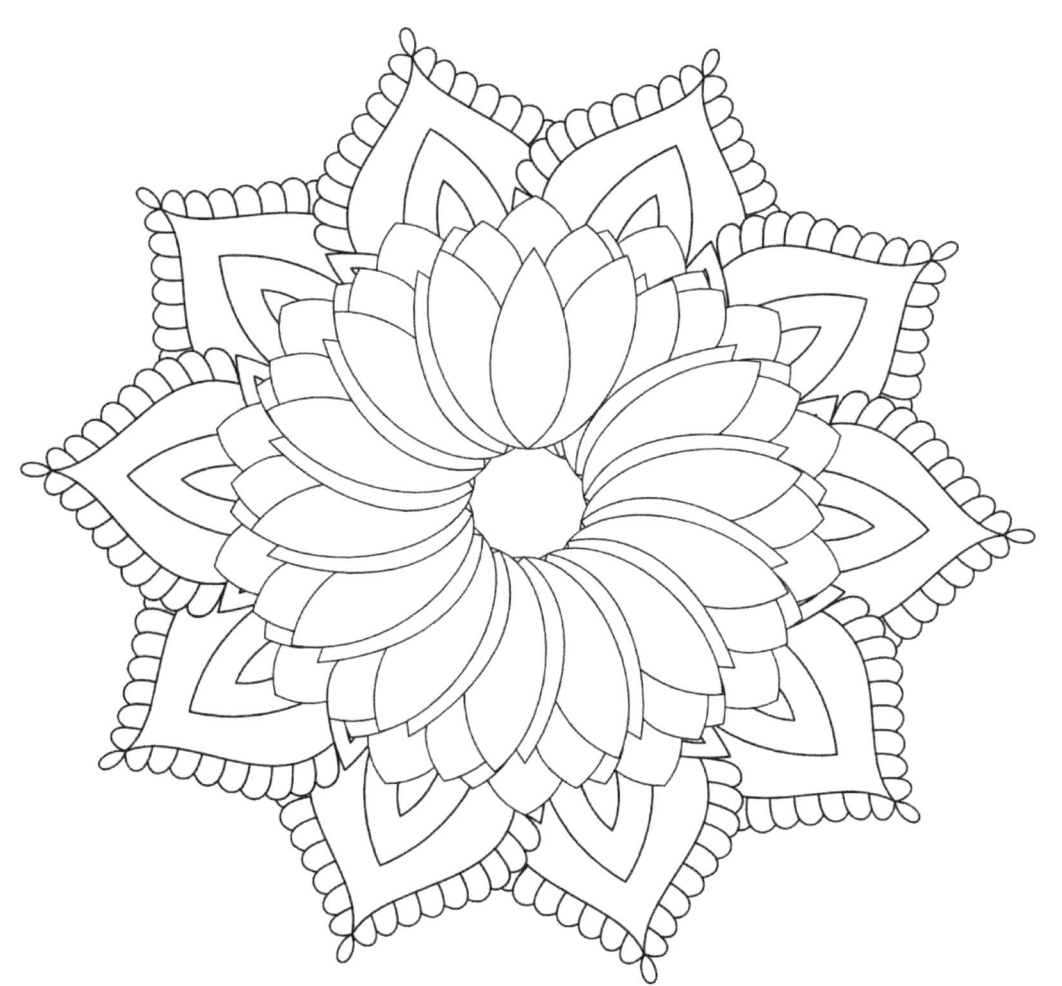

In stillness there is movement.

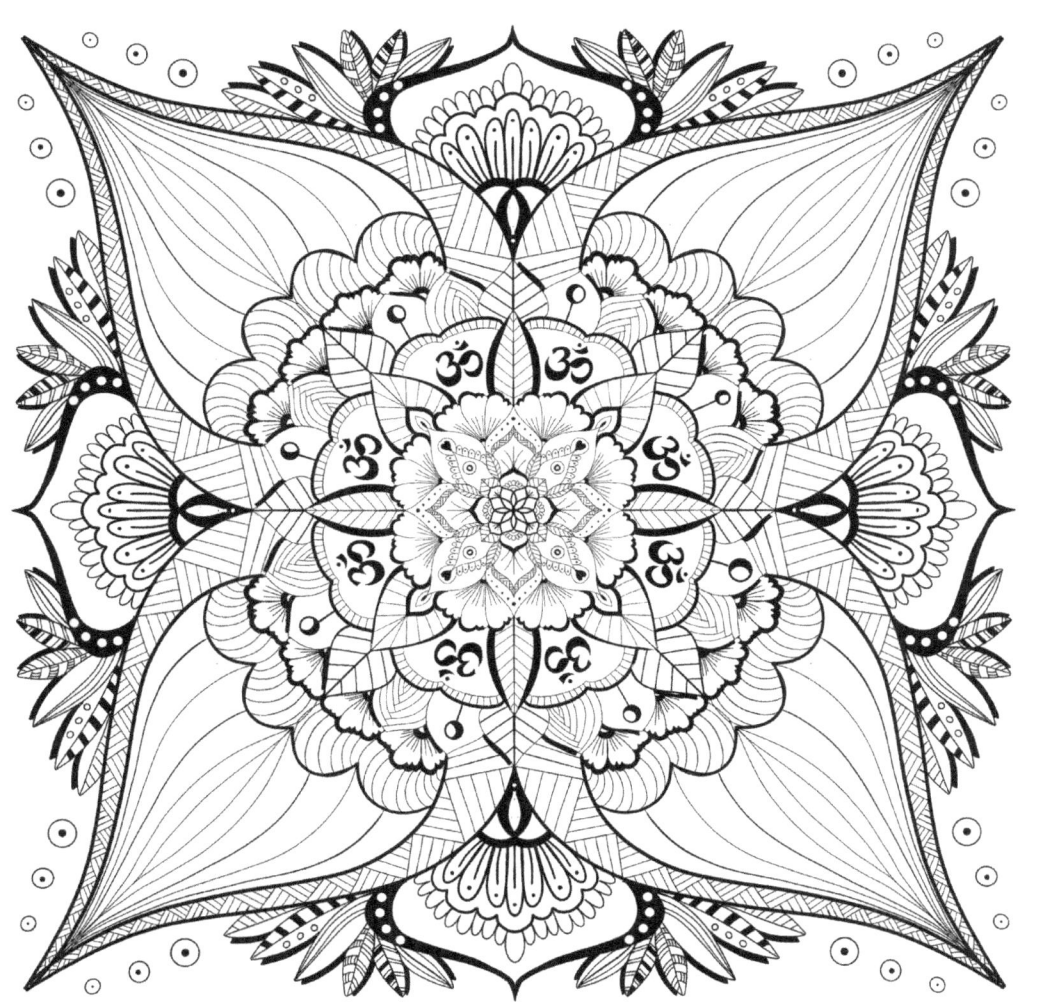

Magic is in the details.

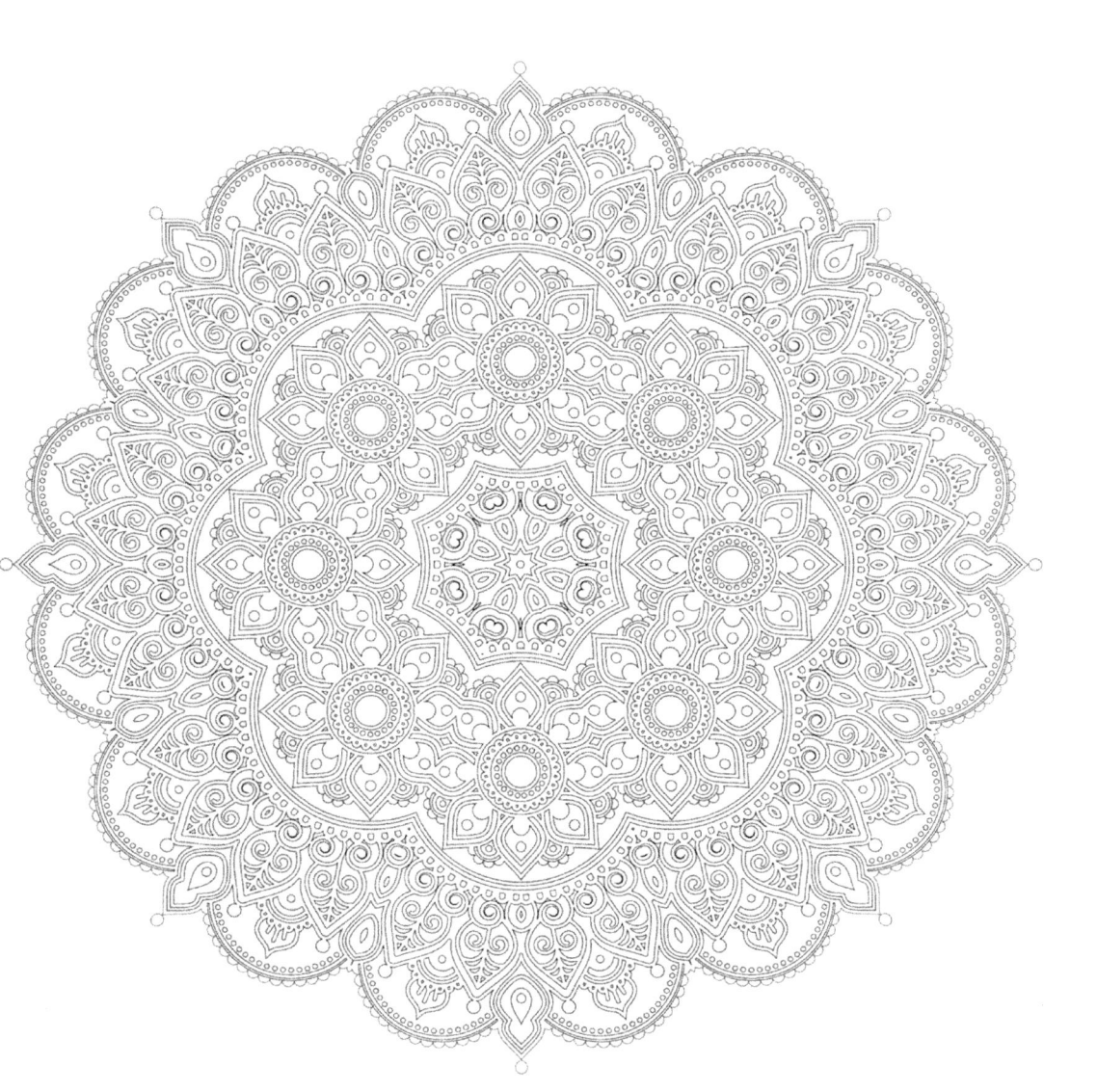

Embrace chaos.

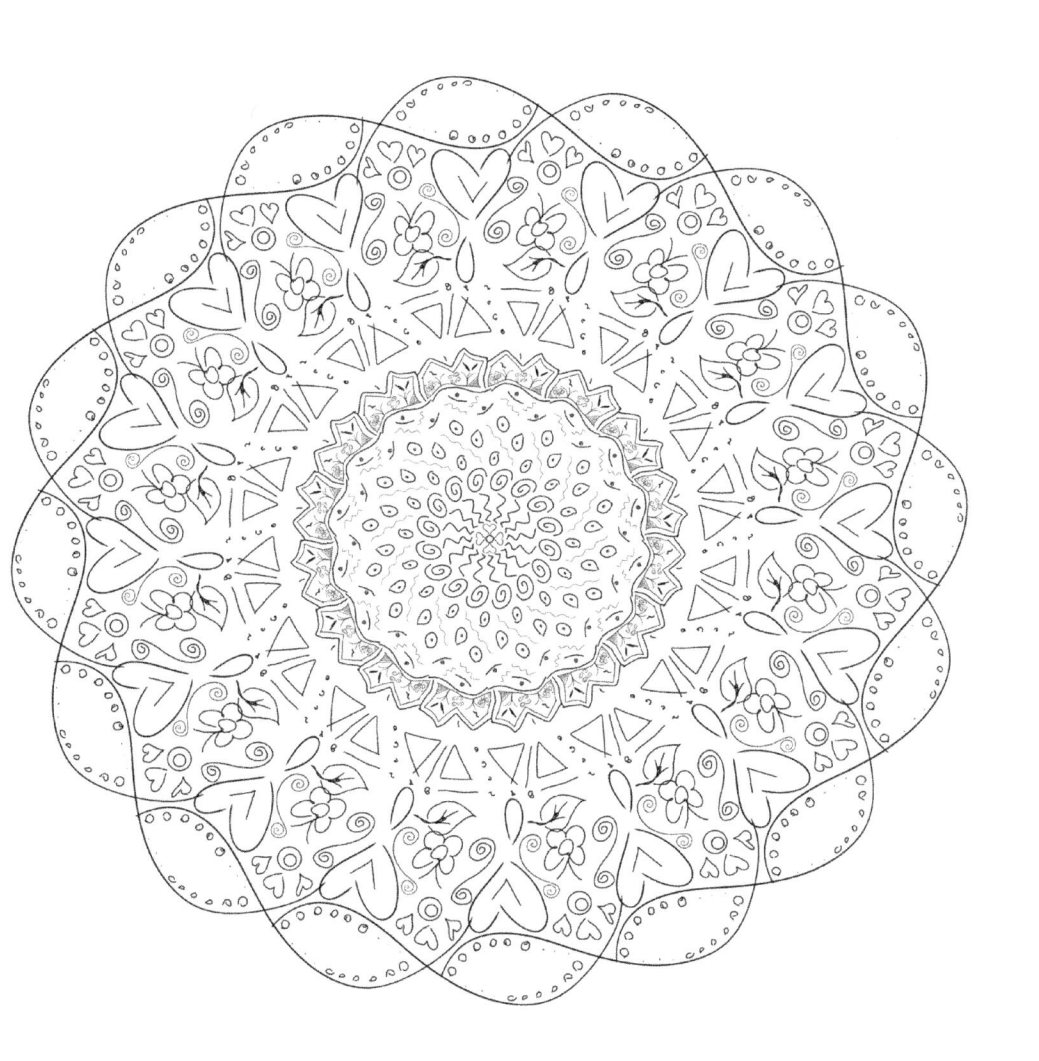

Set the world on fire.

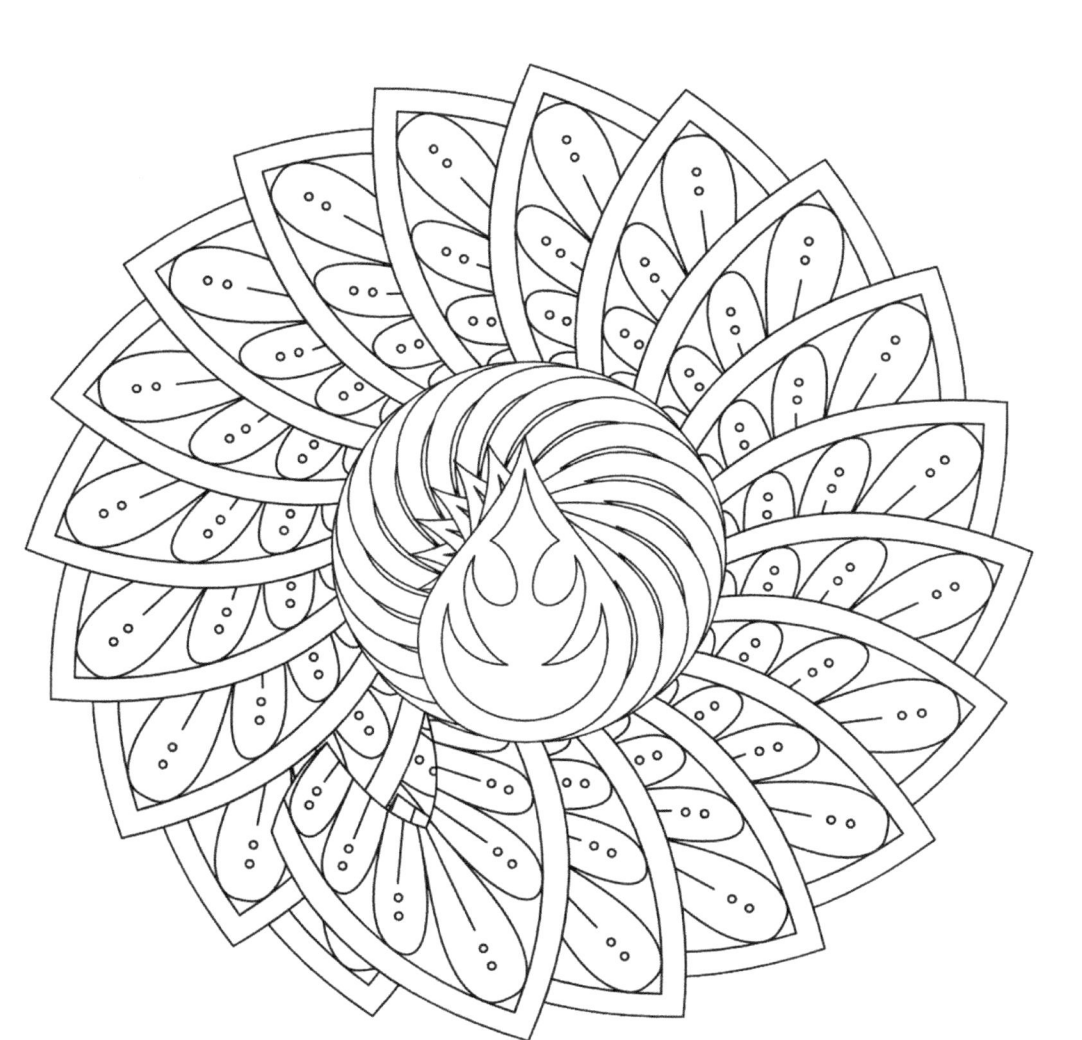

Give birth to good ideas.

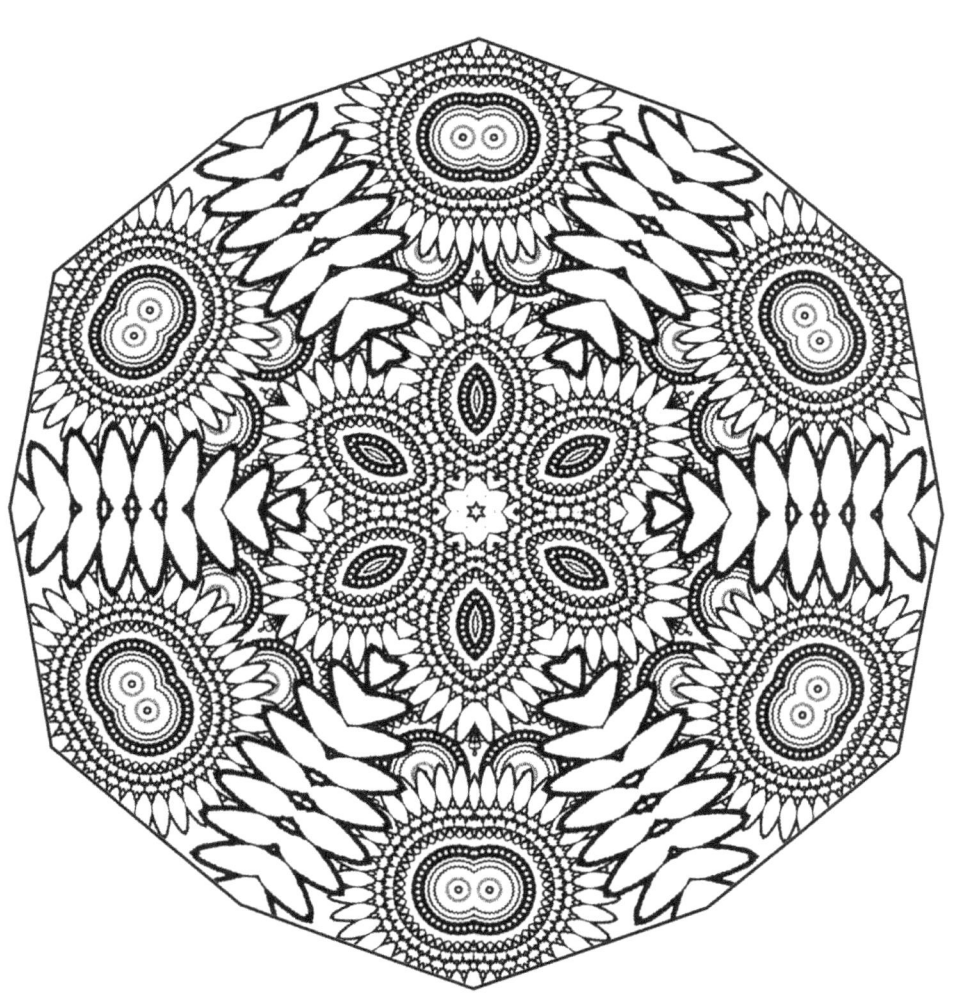

Give it a shake.

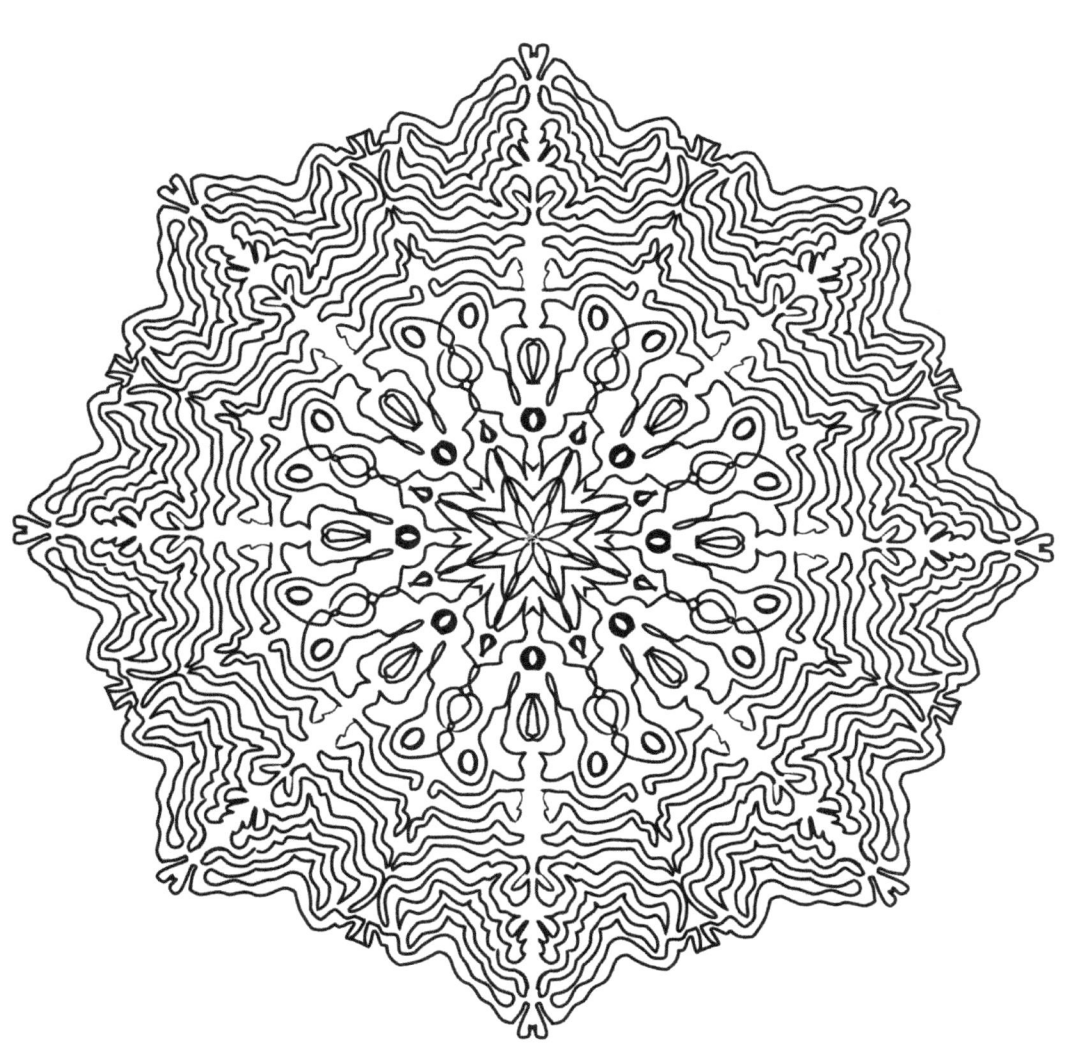

Pick the flowers, there are plenty out there.

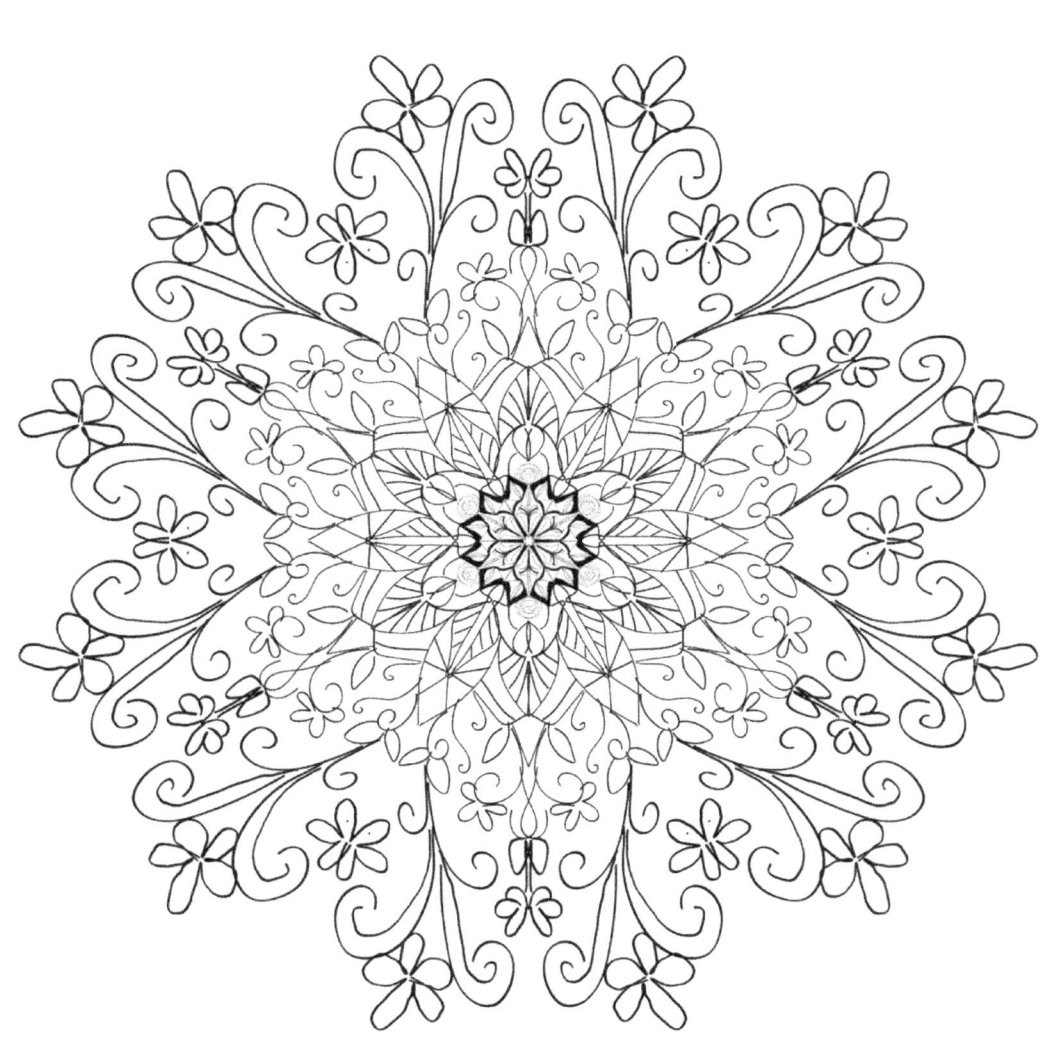

Cultivate creativity.

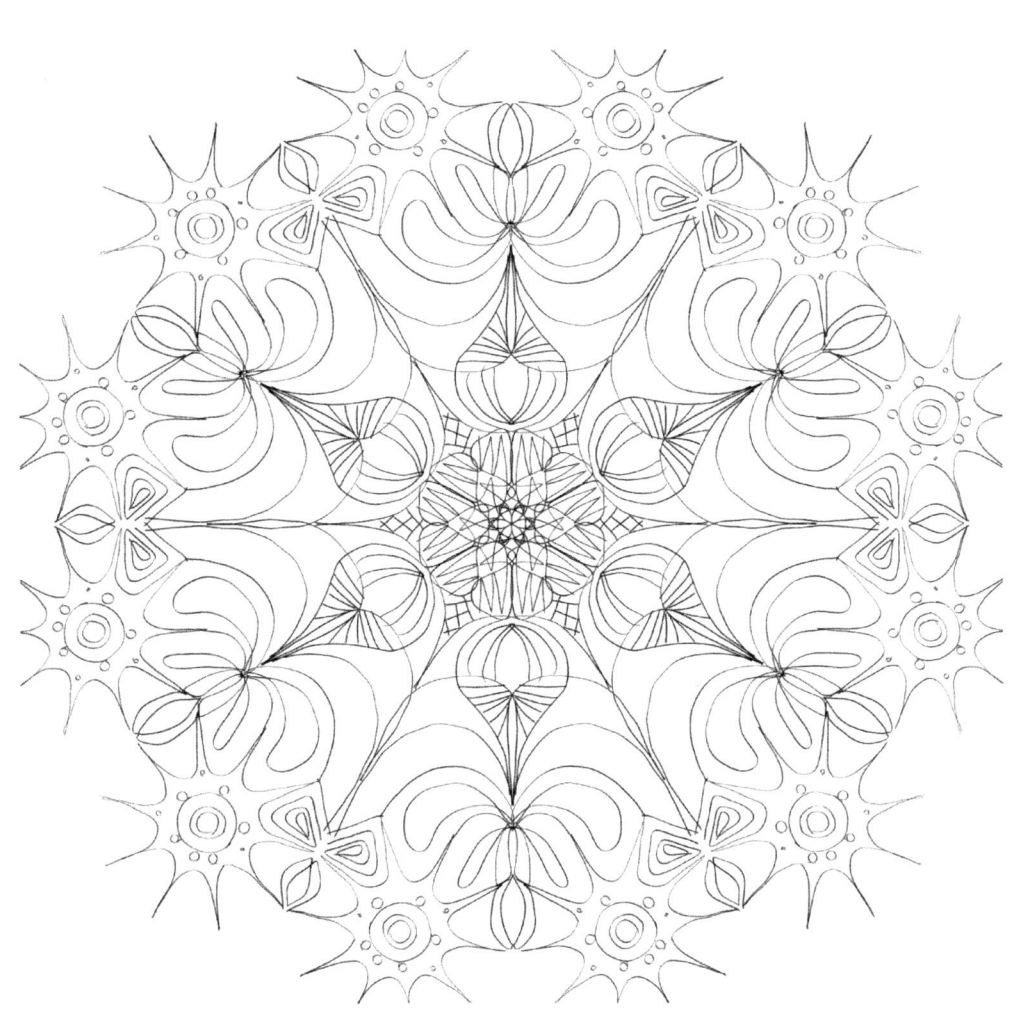

Don't hide yourself.

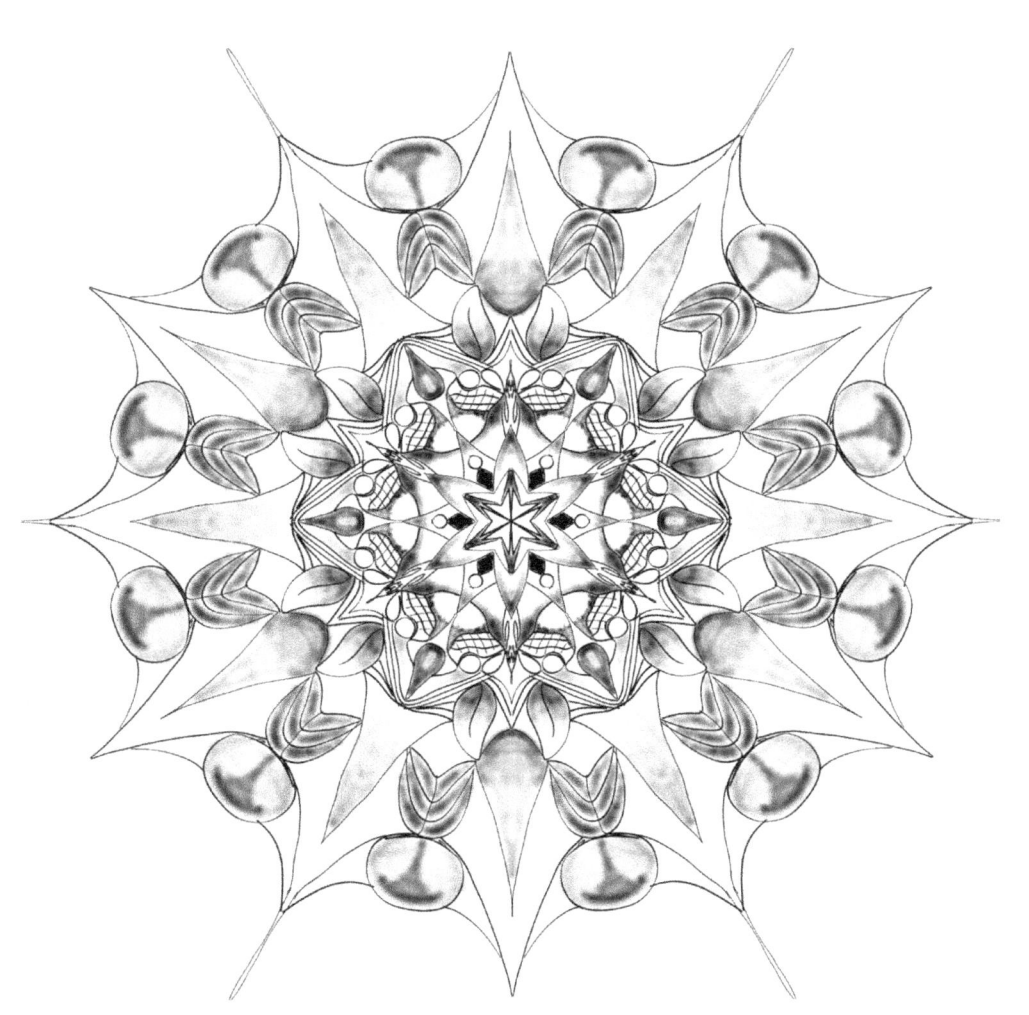

Articulate your ideas.

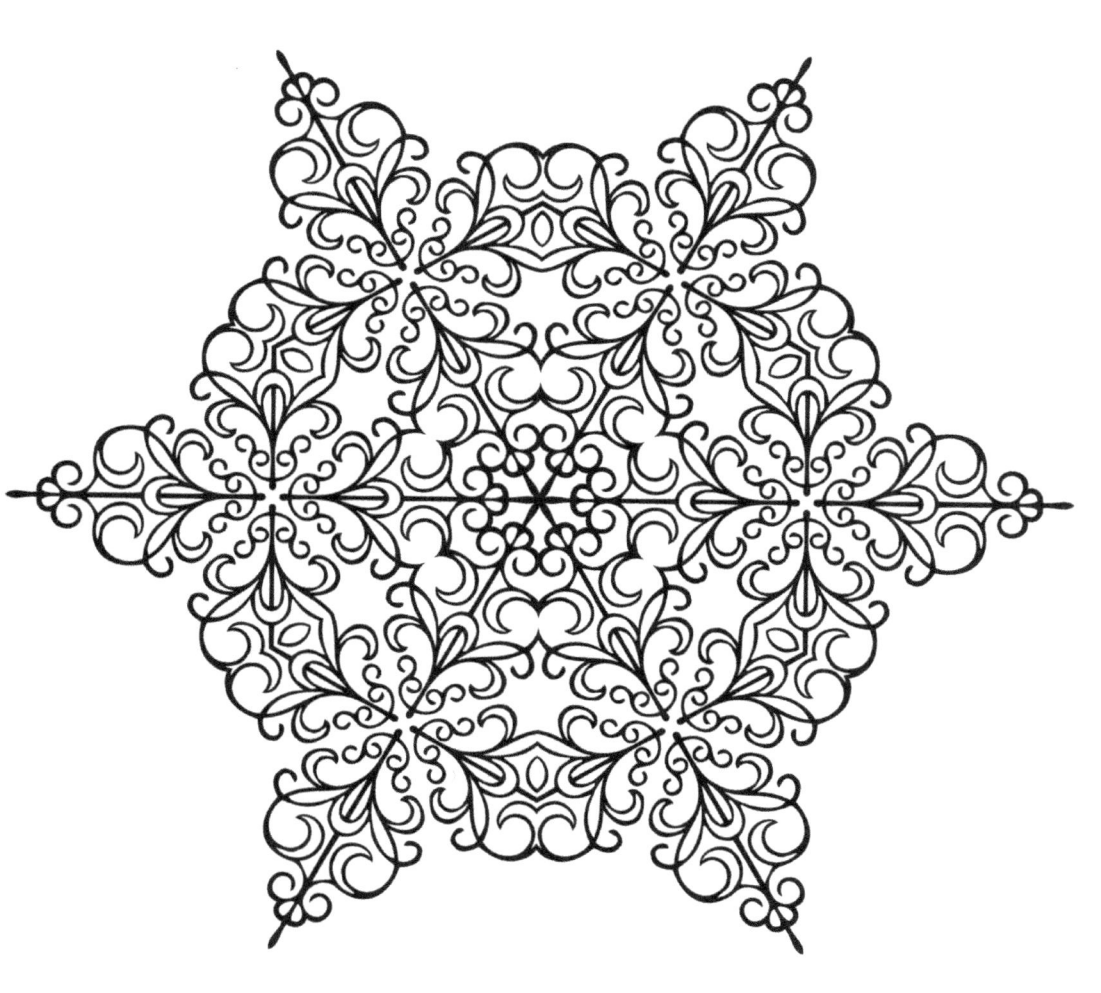

Become a good listener.

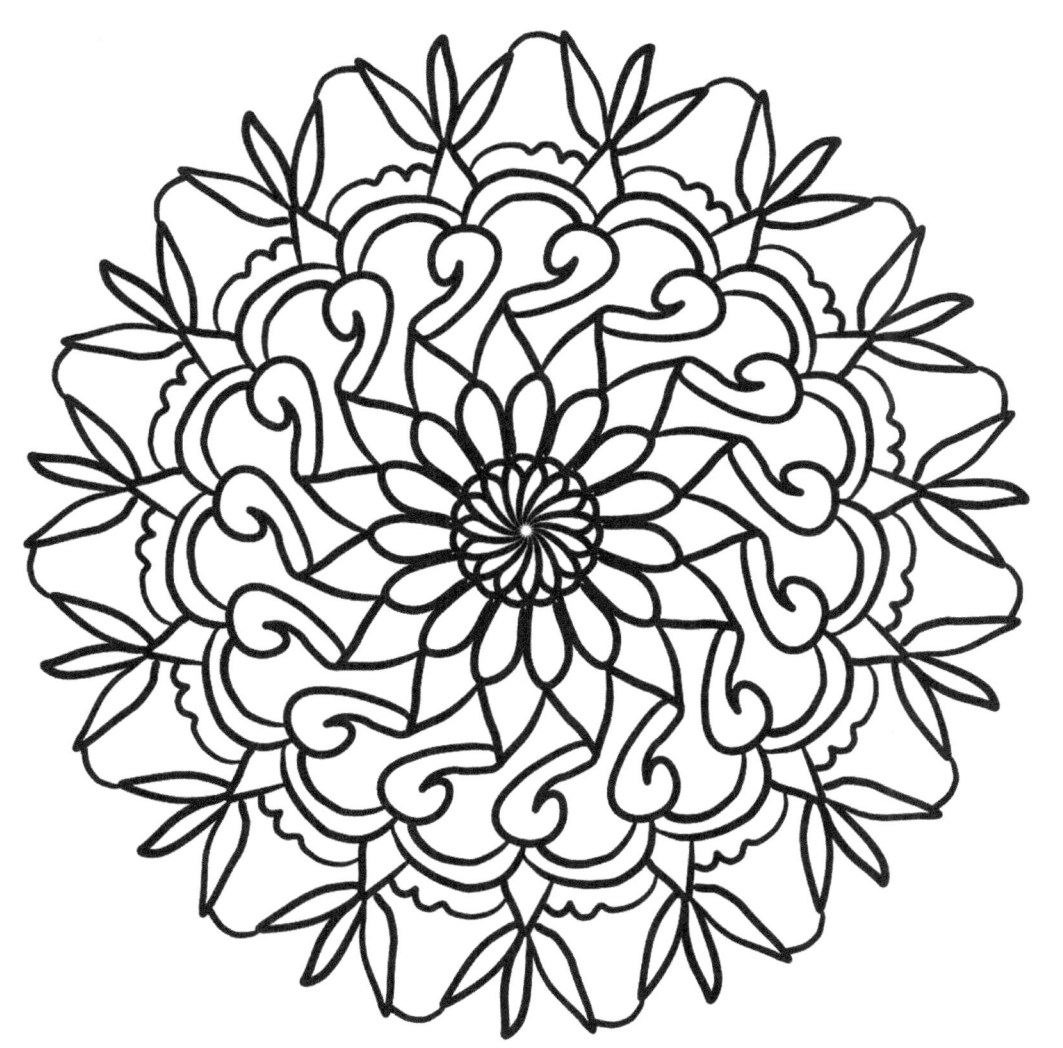

Shape it your way.

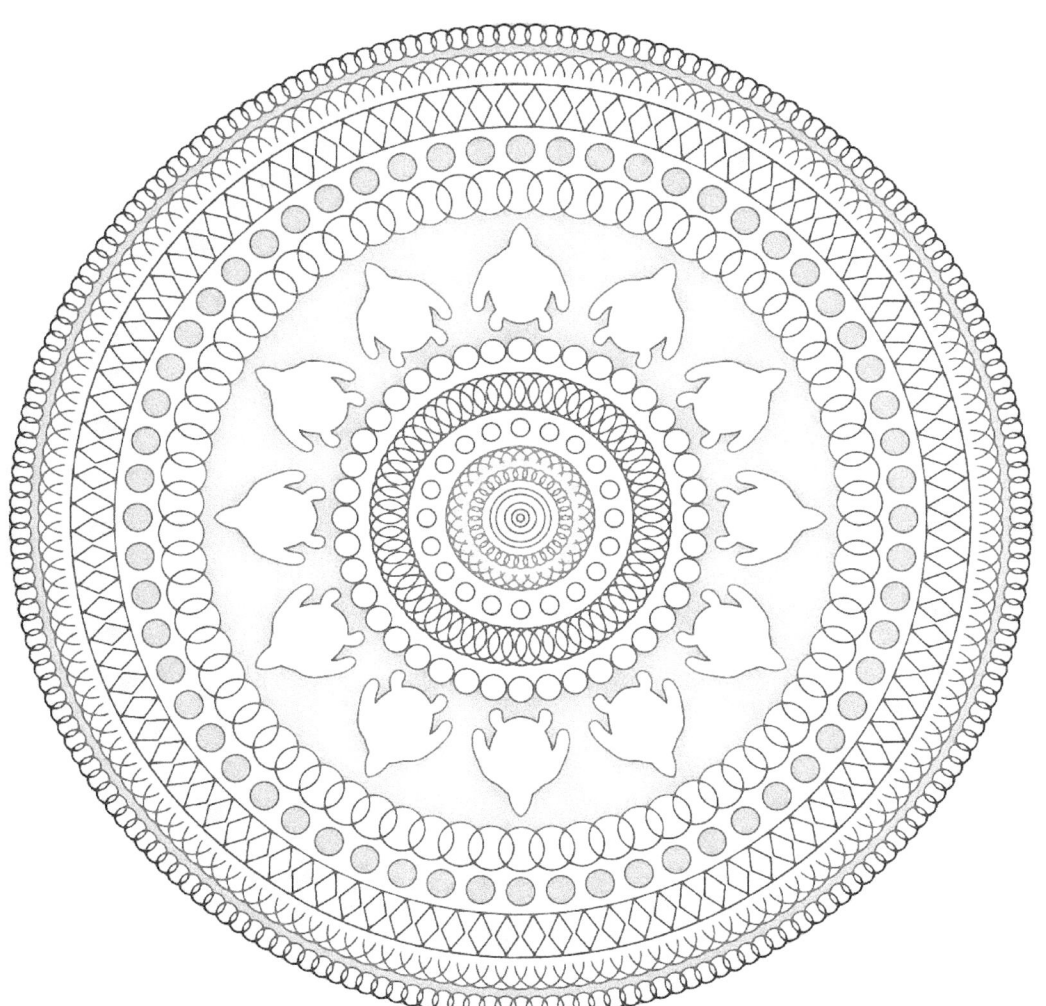

Find the patterns, your comprehension will improve.

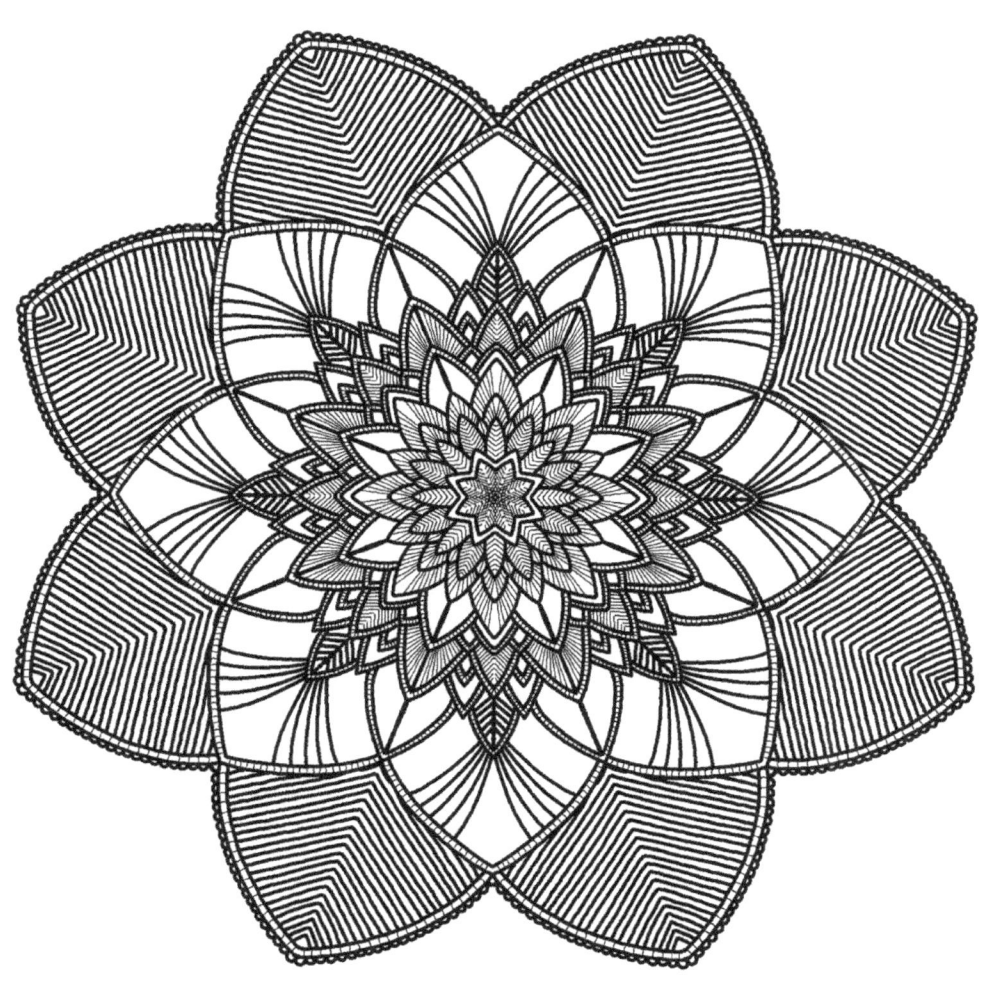

Crack the shell.

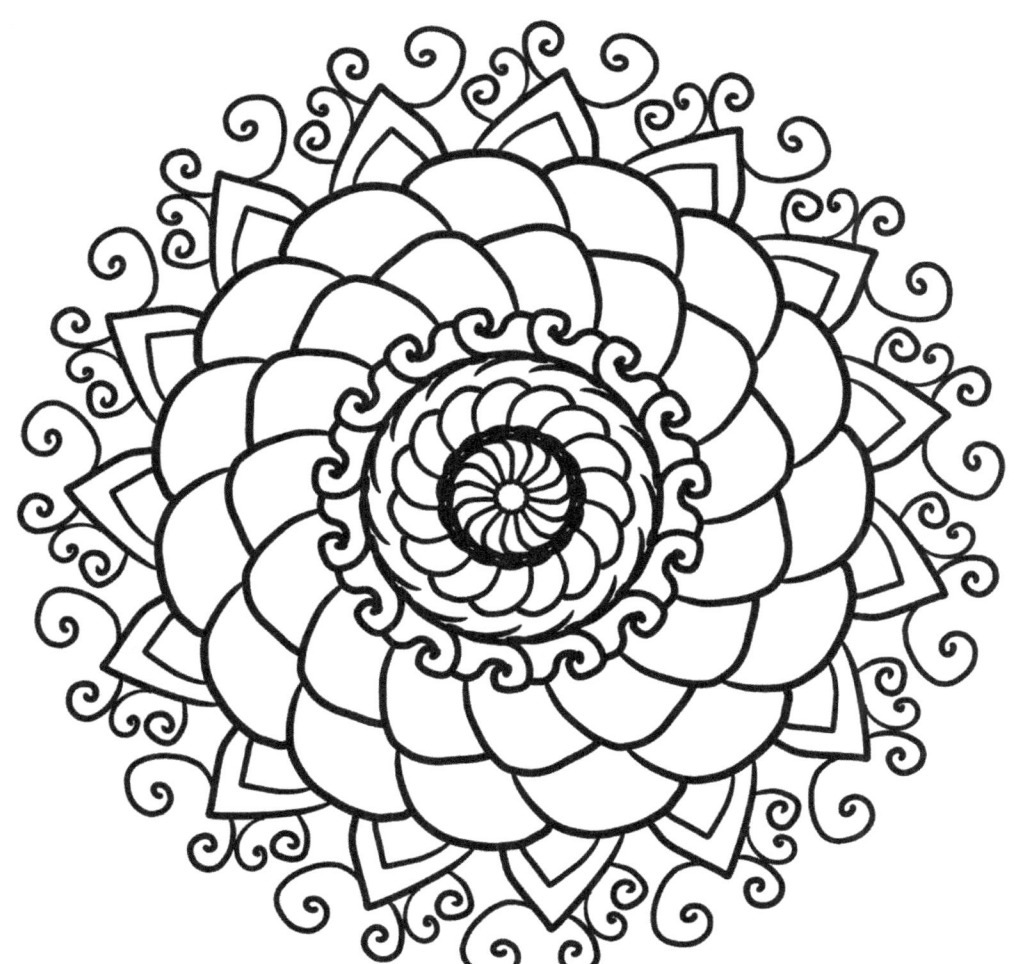

Bounce back from failure.

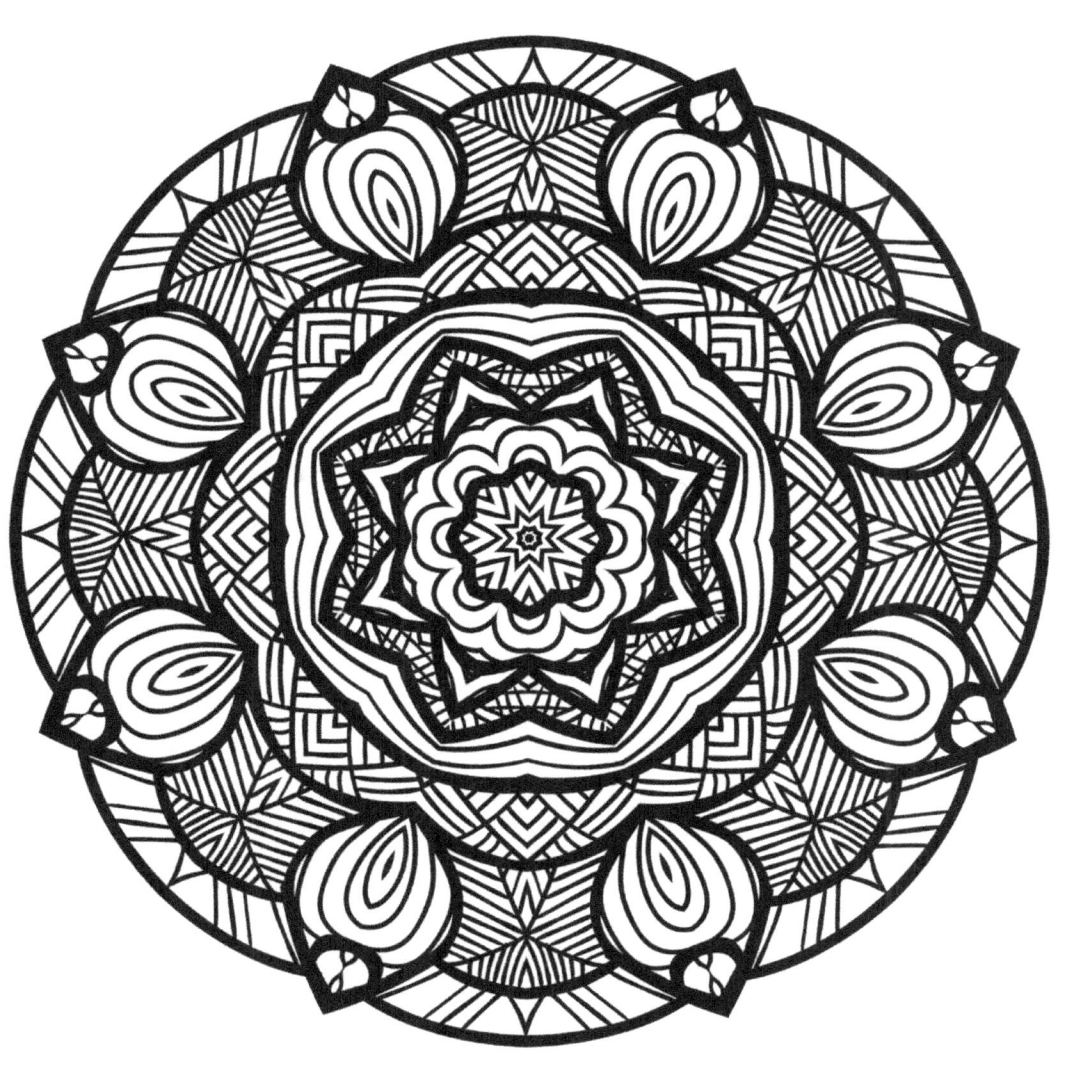

To become free, put some limits.

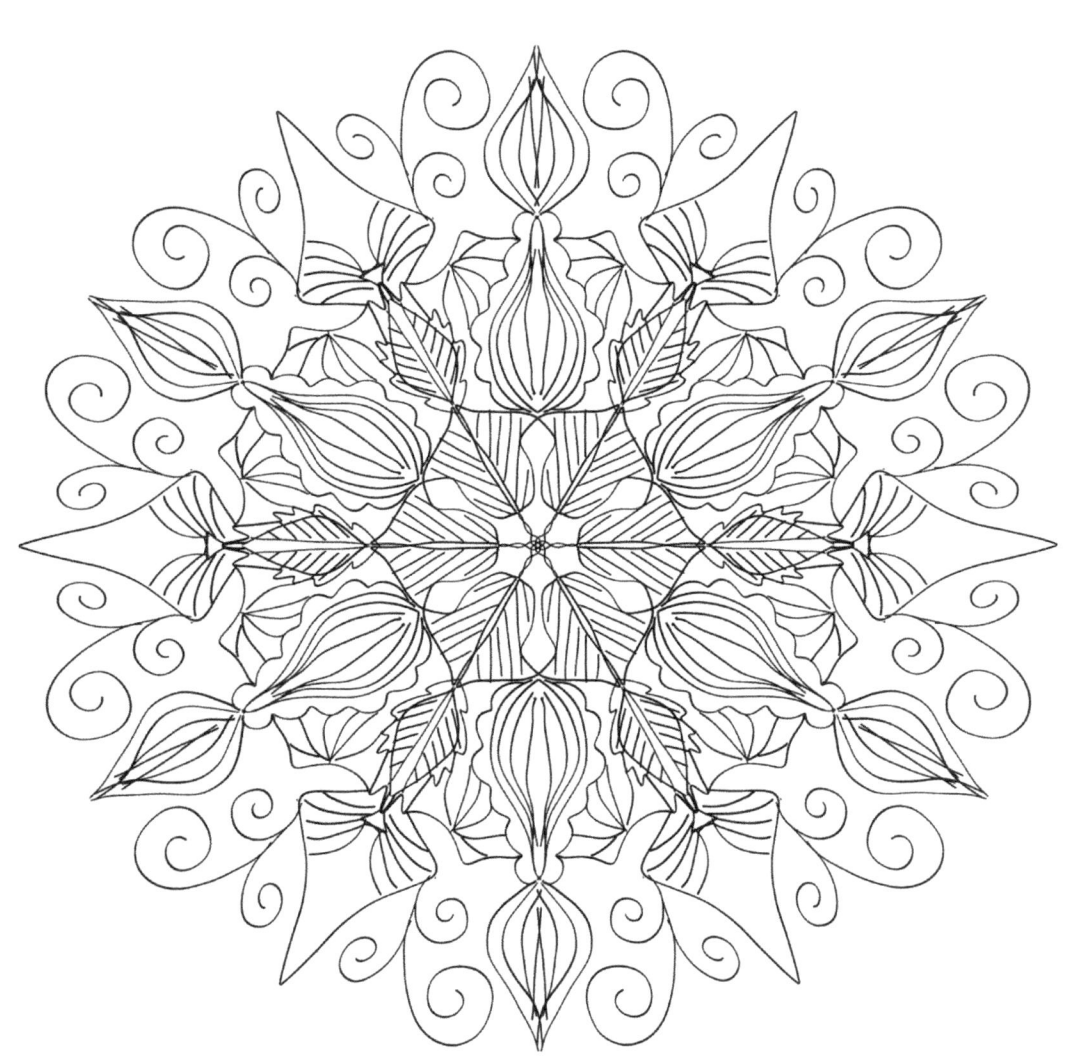

In a world where you can be anything, be kind.

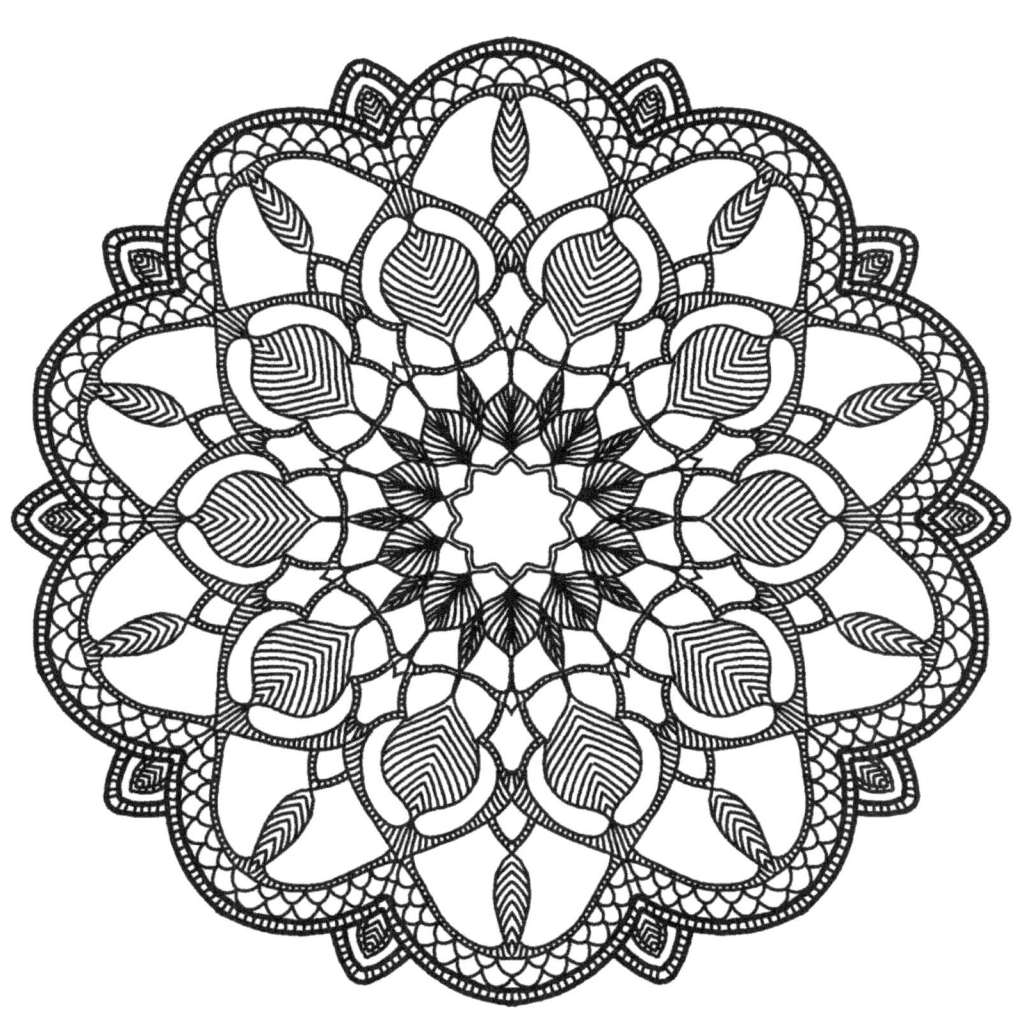

Discover your core values.

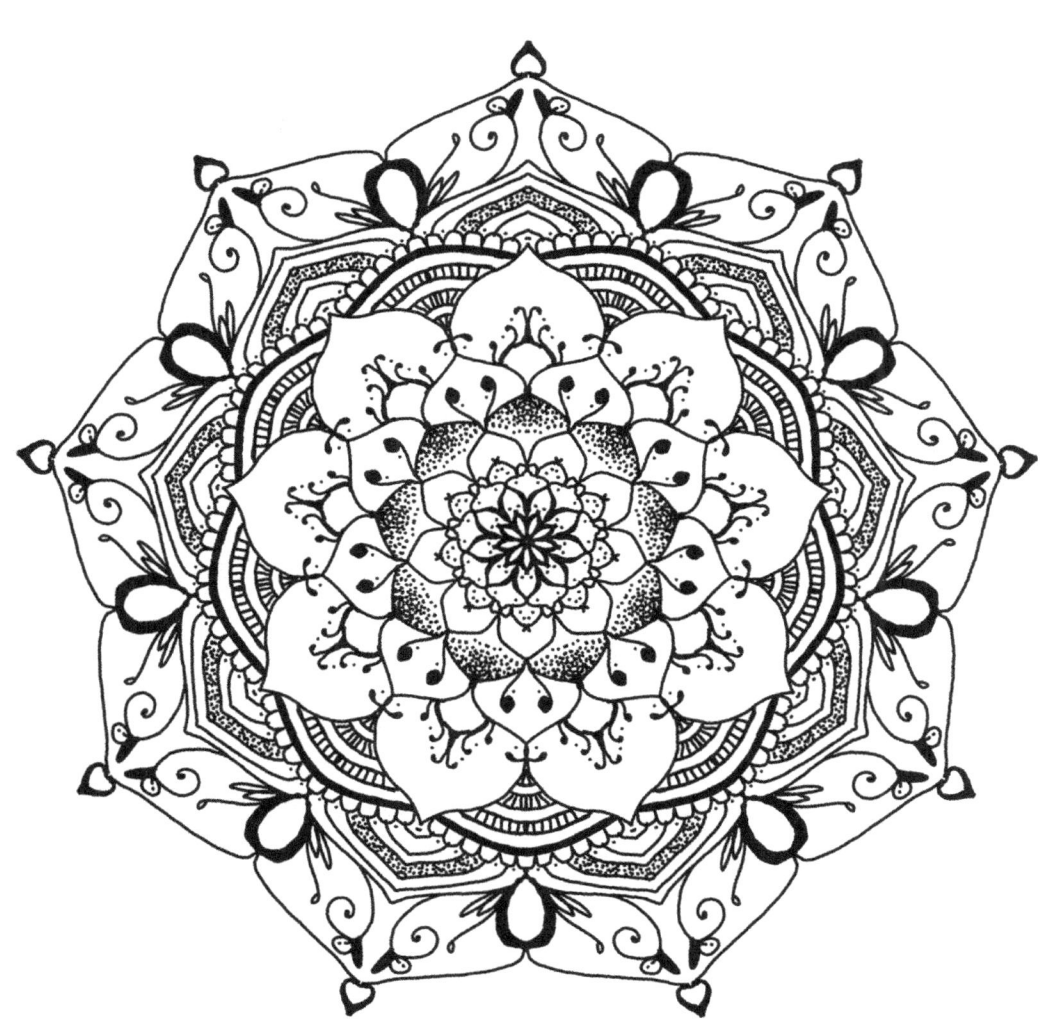

Let it go.

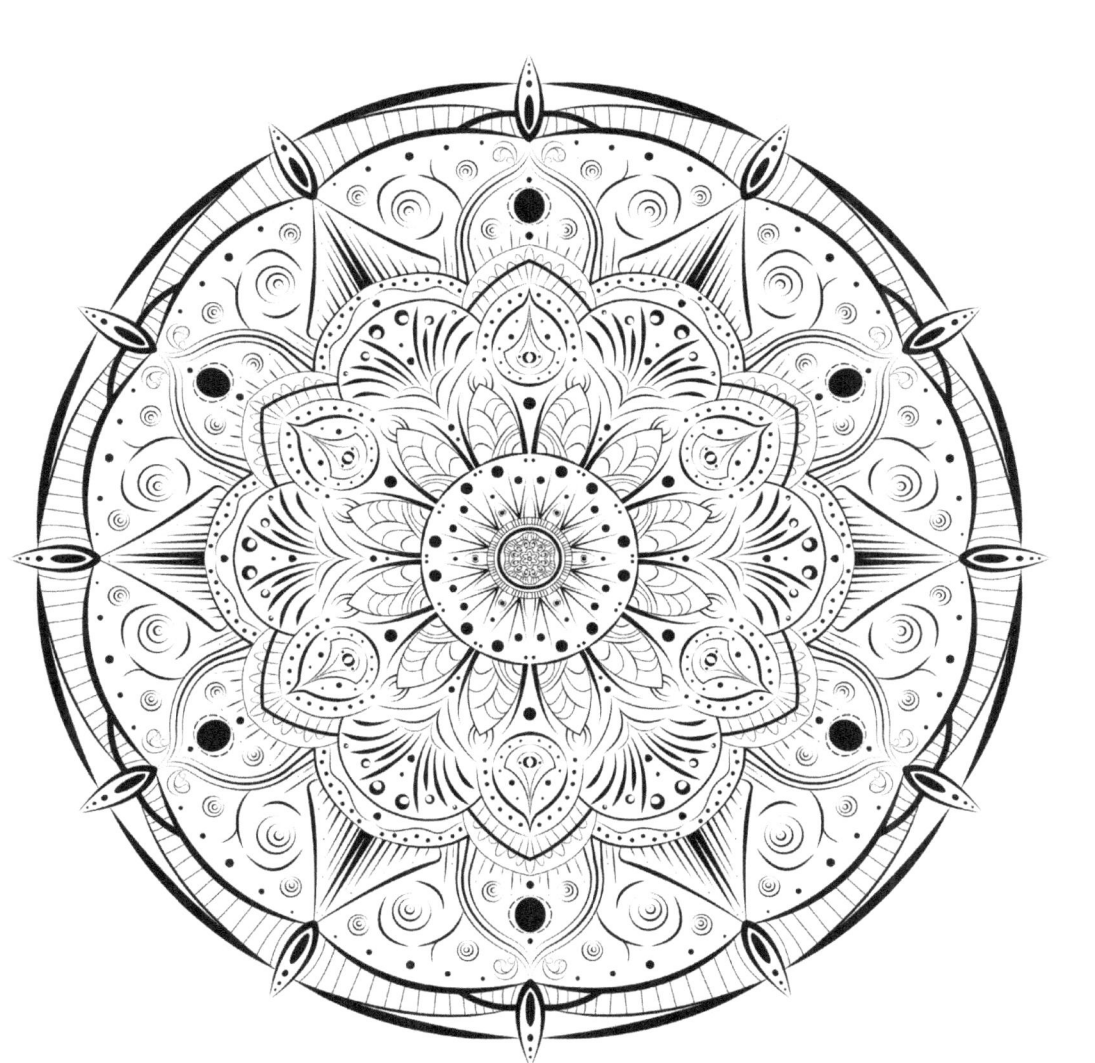

Work harder on yourself than you do on your job.

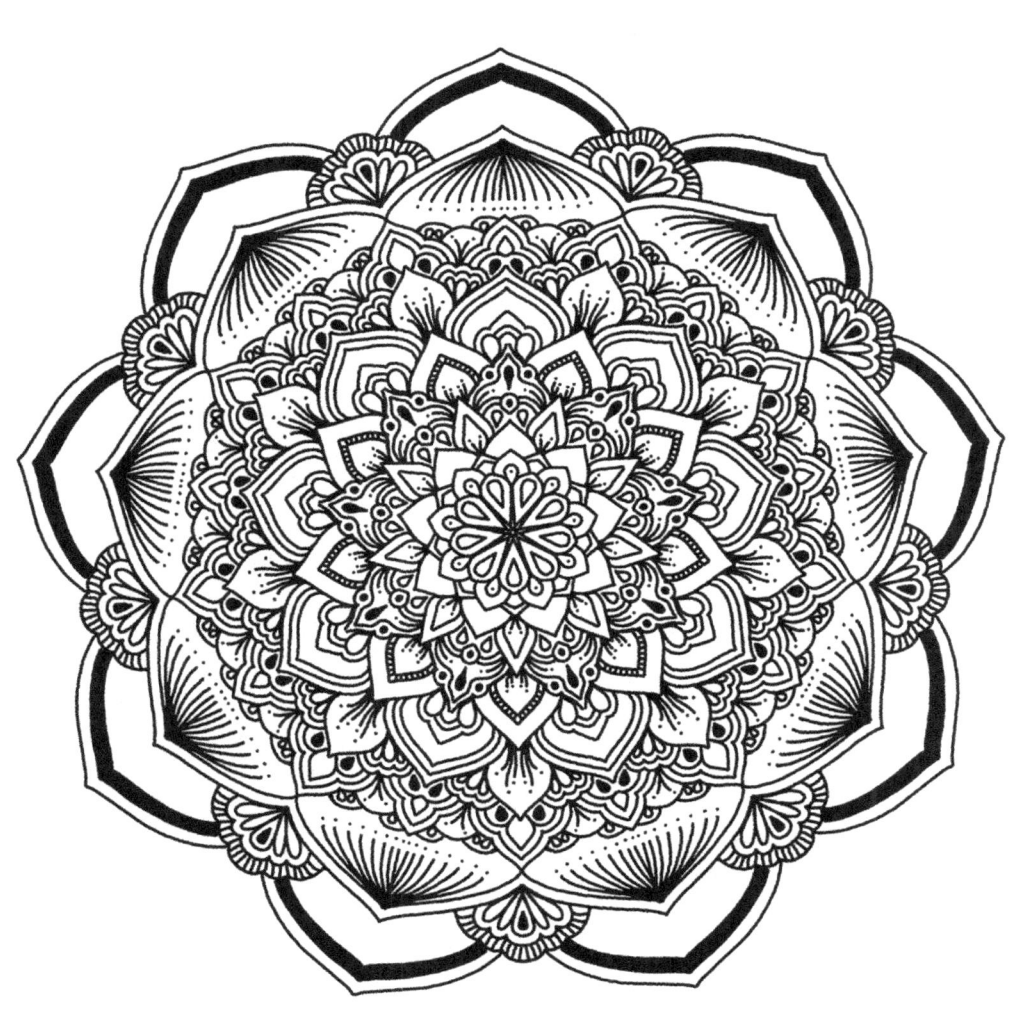

Stay minimalist.

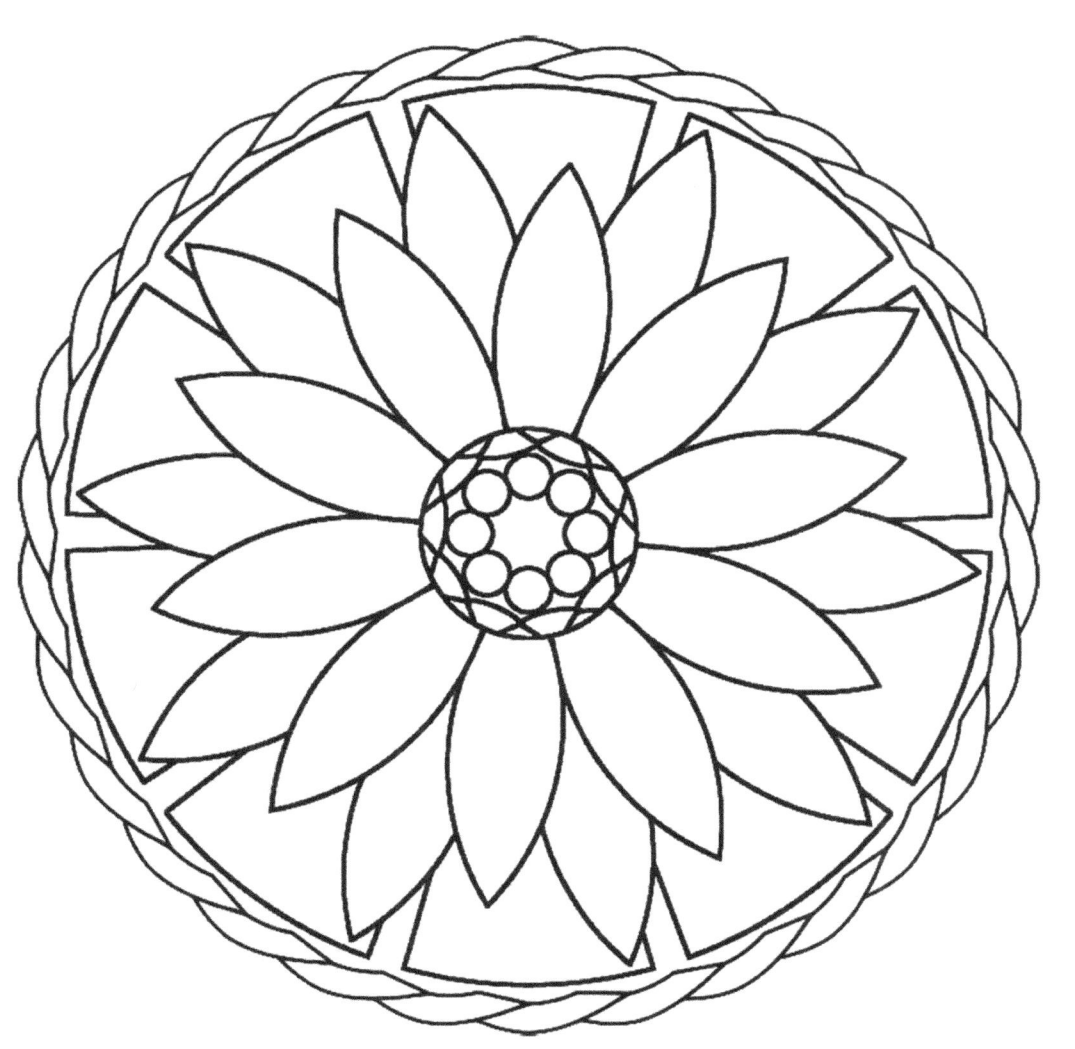

Explore the dark.

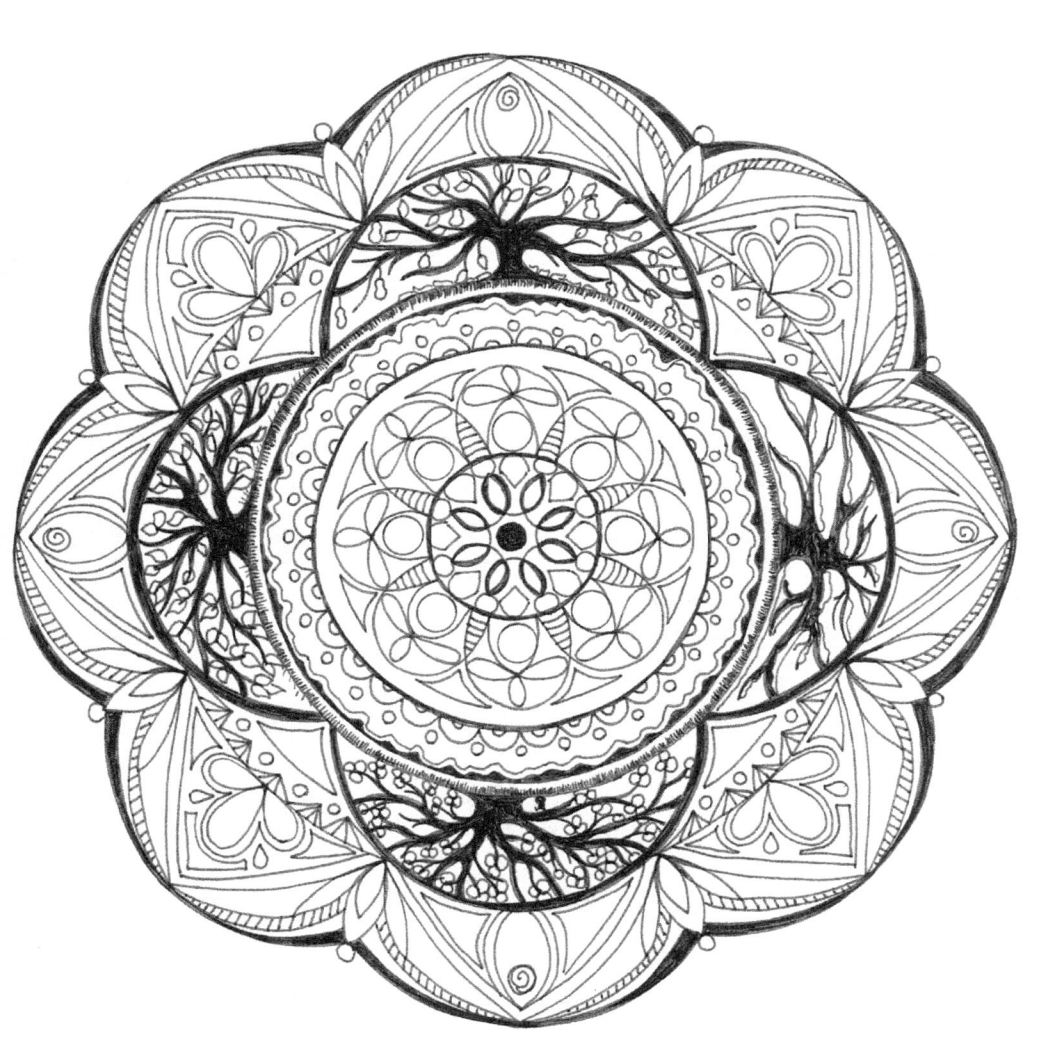

Strengthen the net.

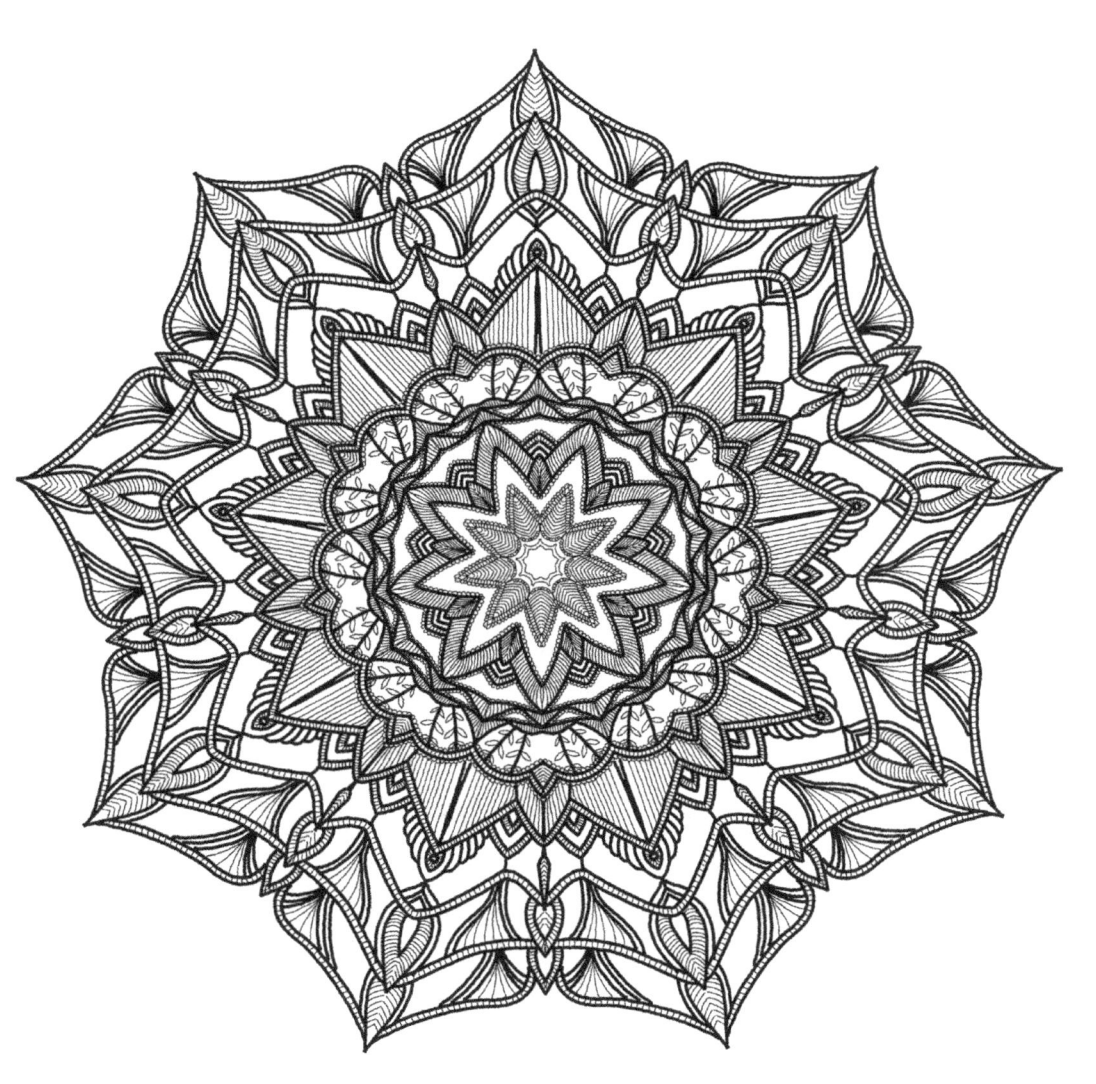

Learn to equalize.

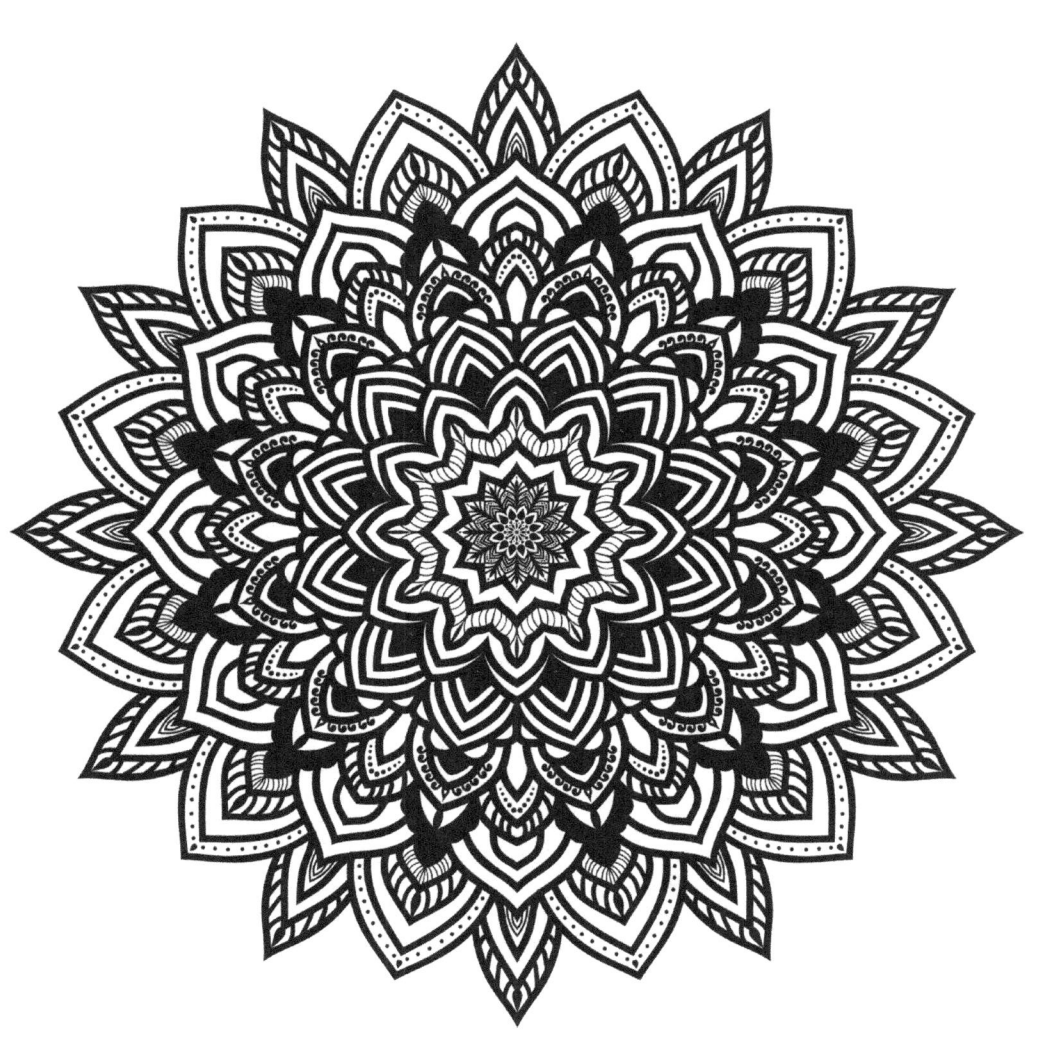

Think about your origins.

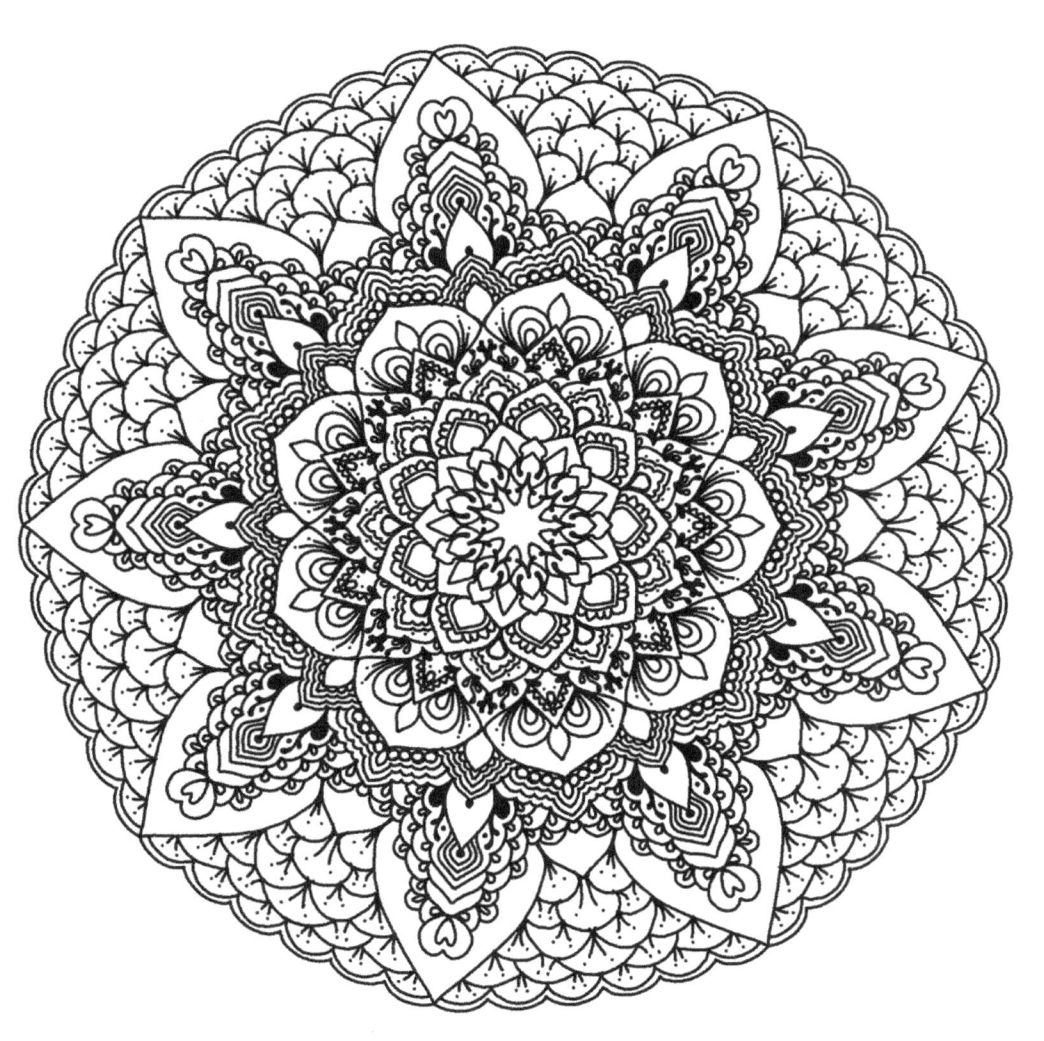

Where do you want to start?

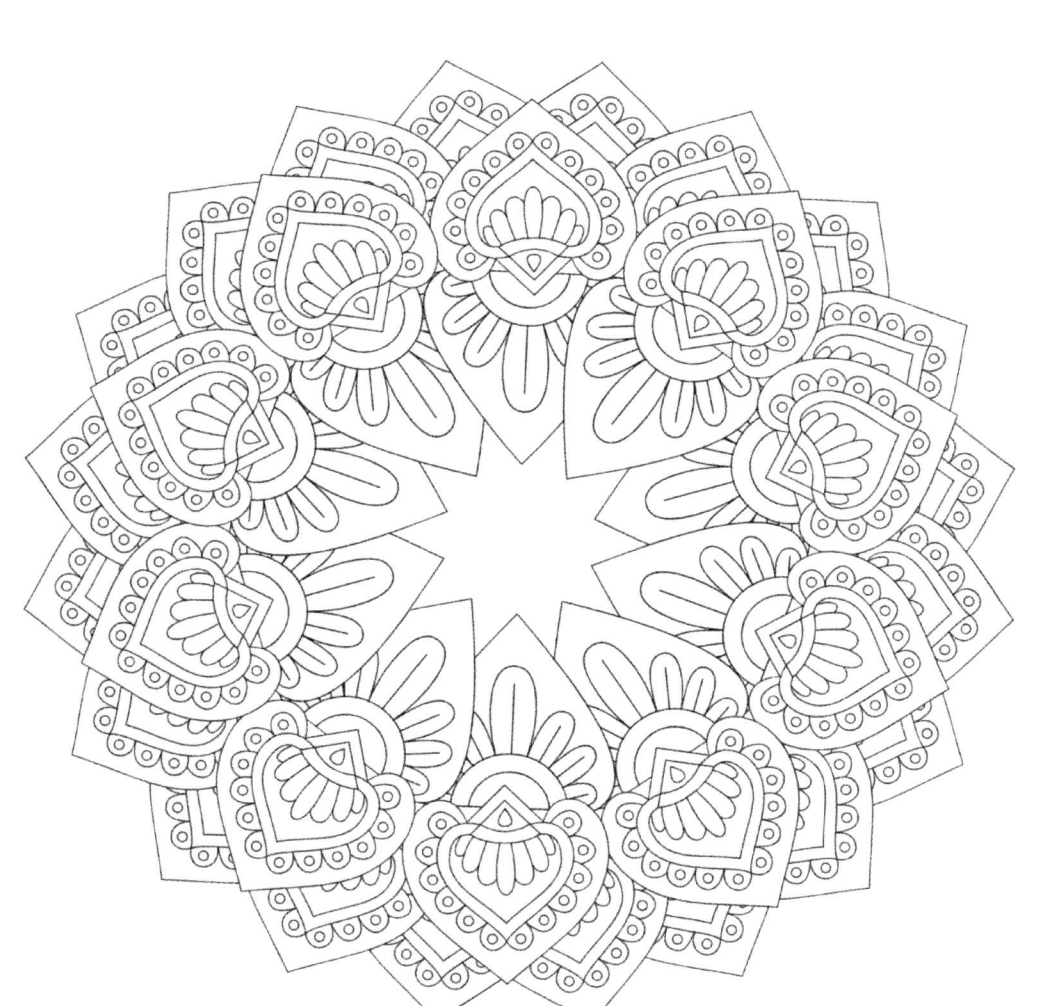

Sometimes you have to cross the line.

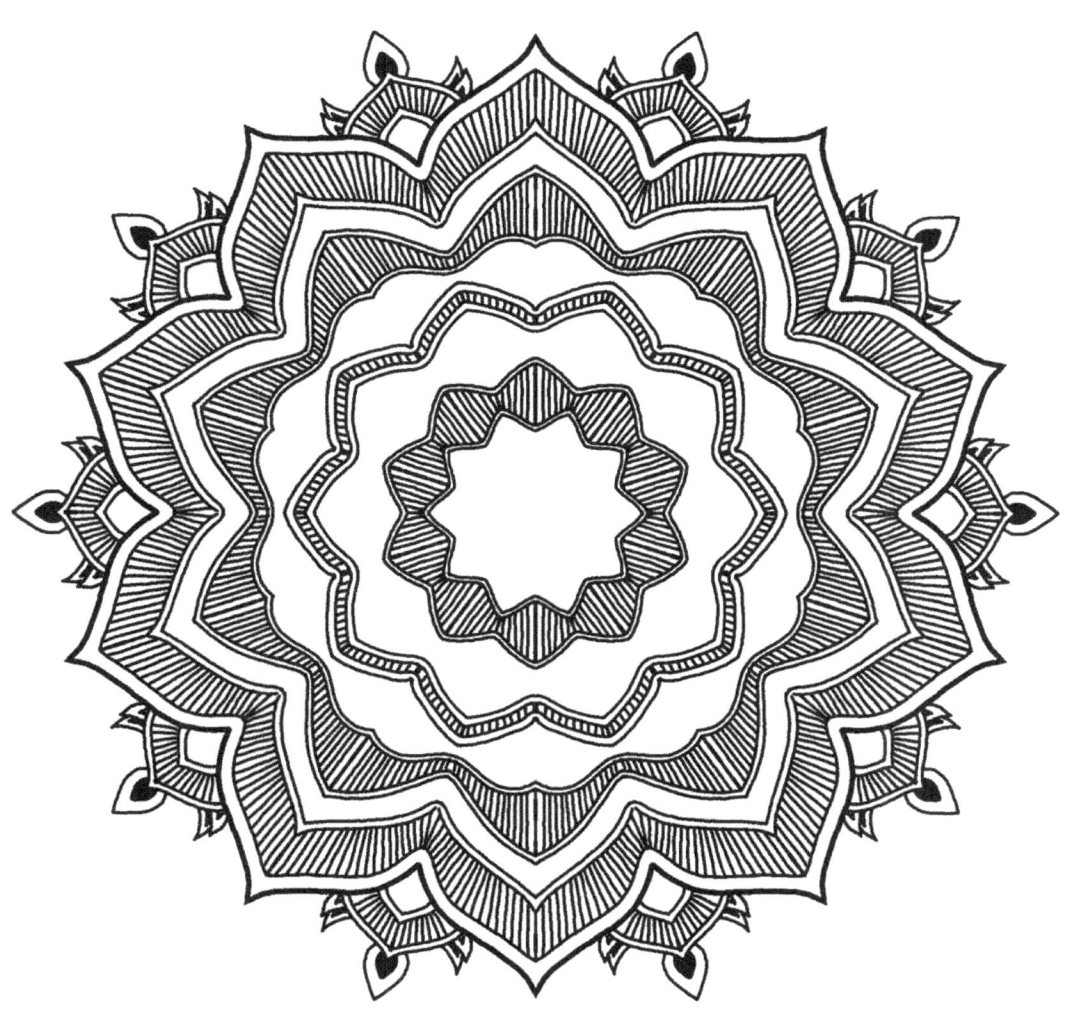

Overlap the known and the unknown.

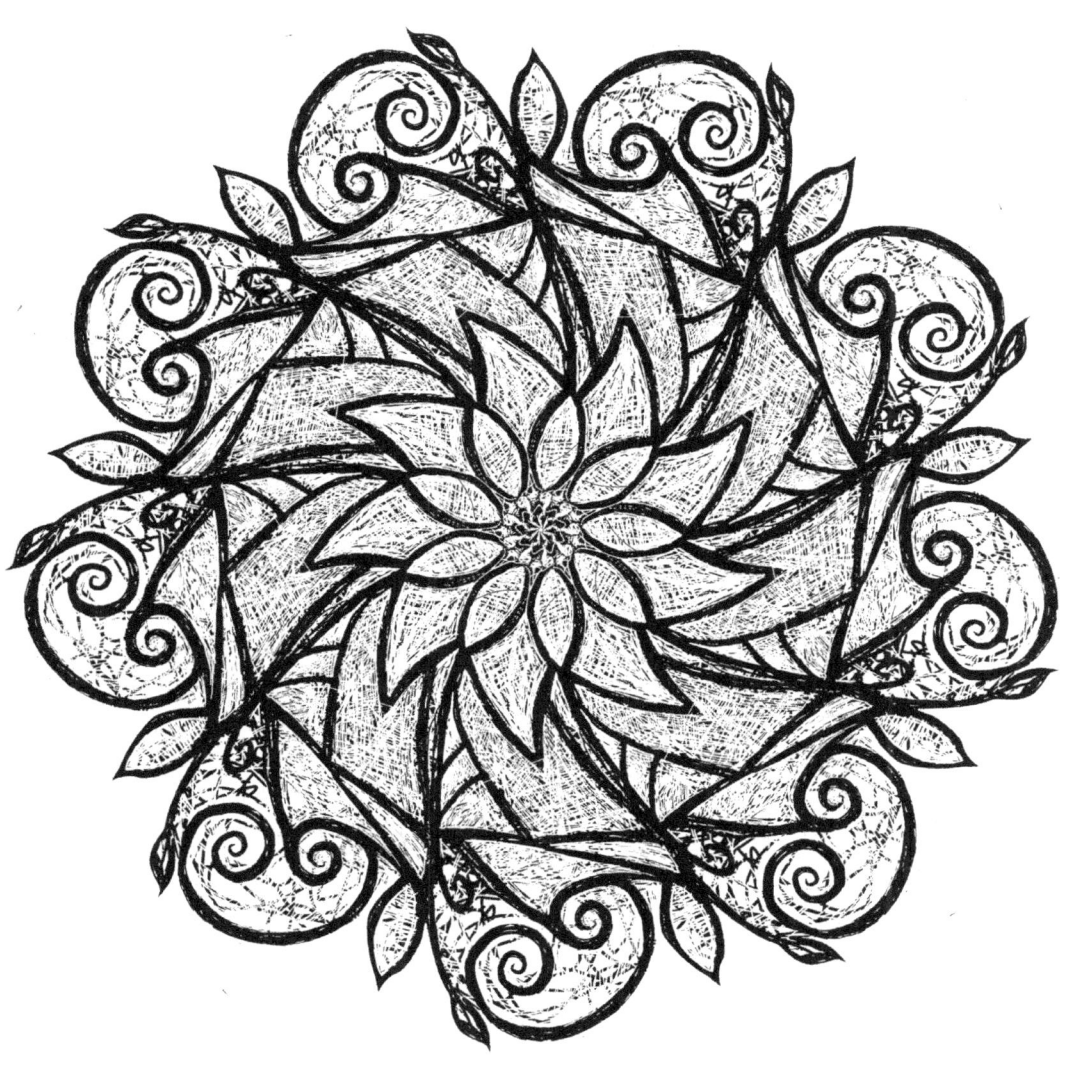

Spread the seeds.

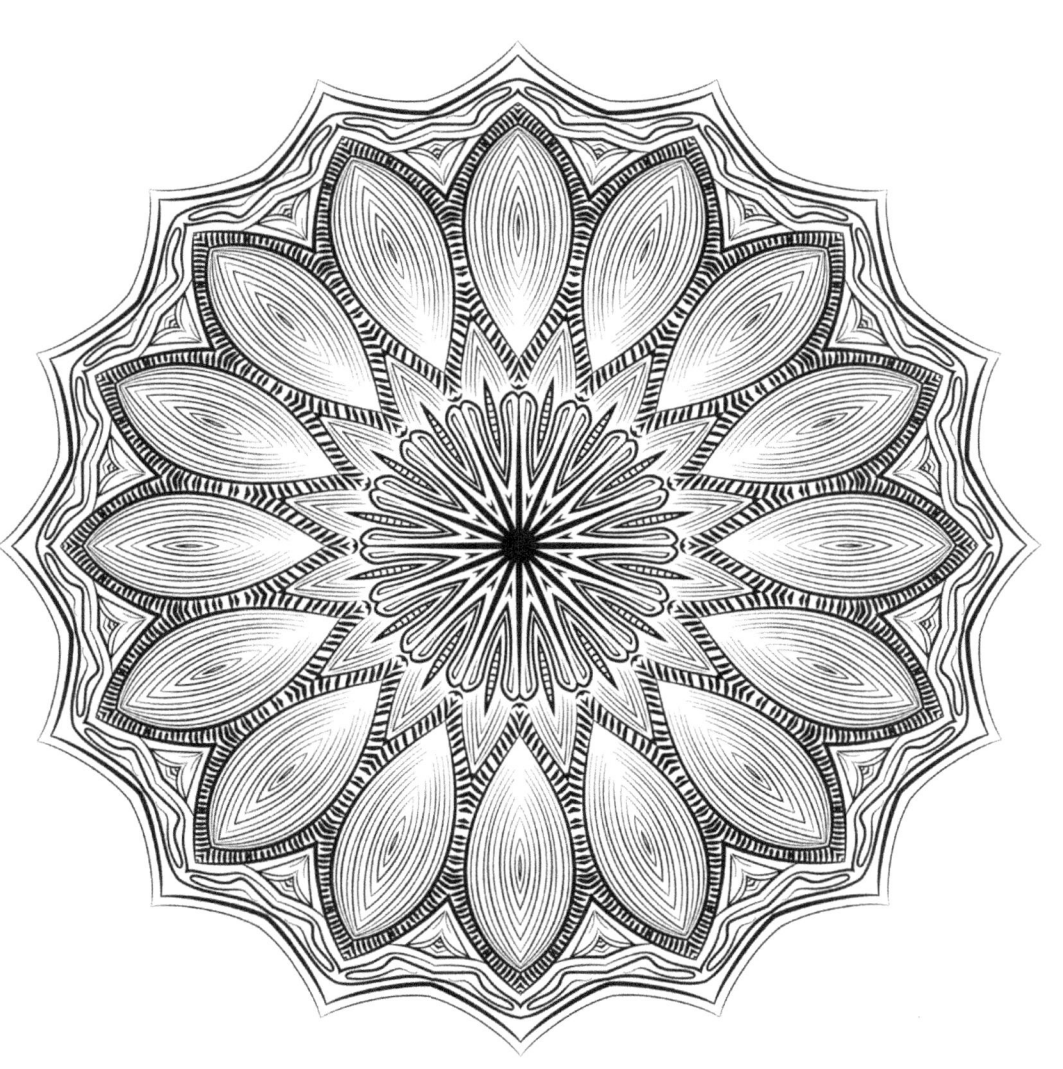

Before judging, look at things from another's perspective.

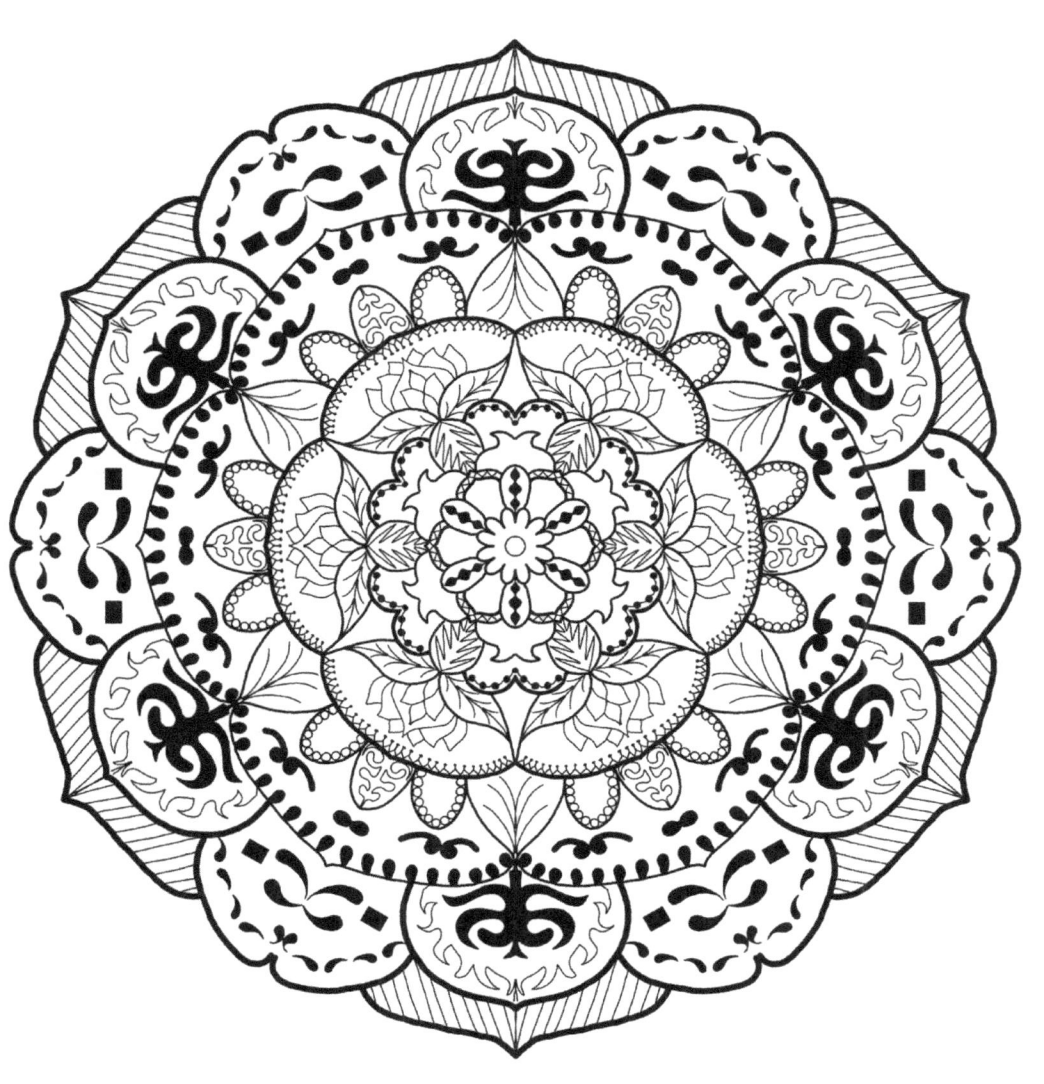

How many cards in your life deck?

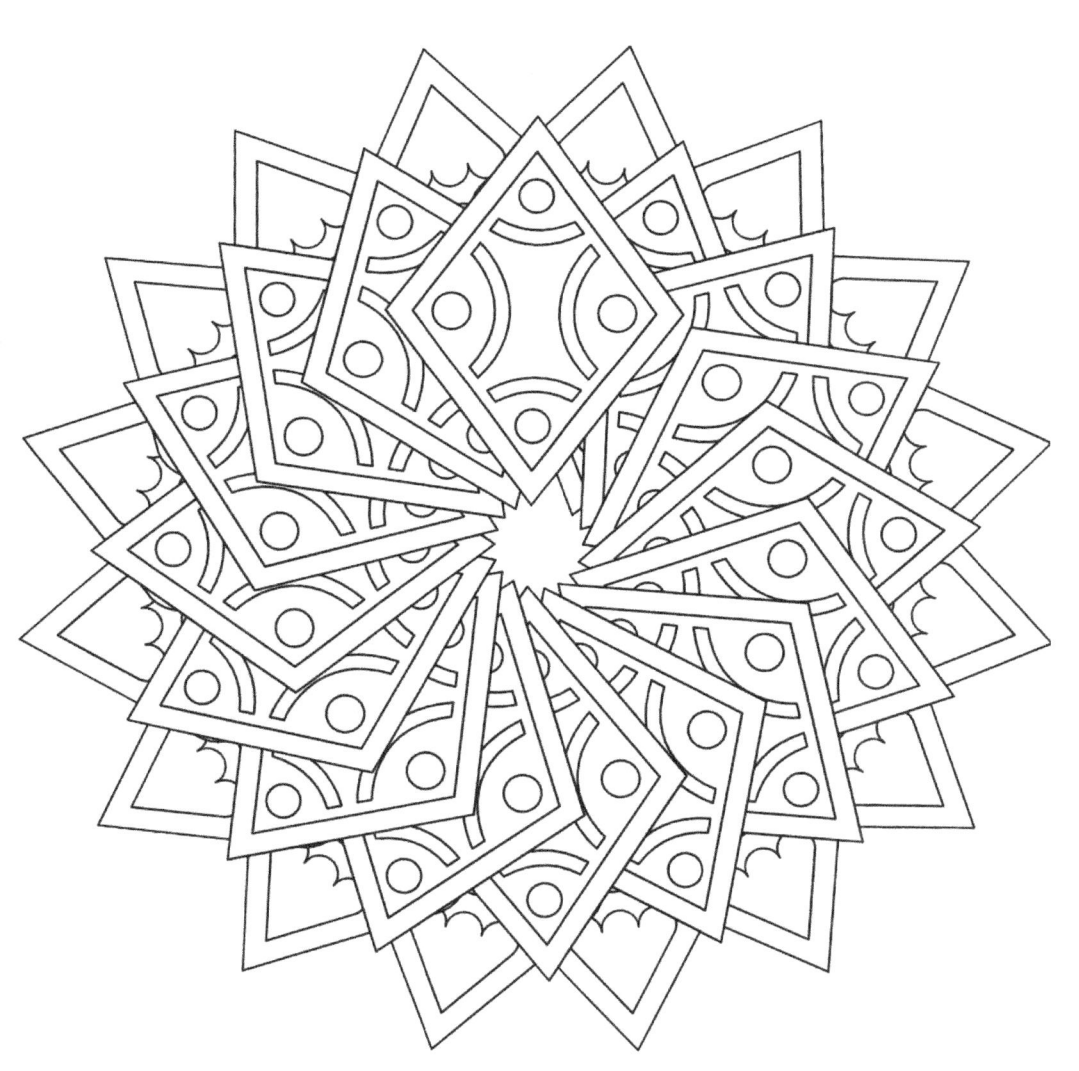

In moments of indecision, let the wheel decide.

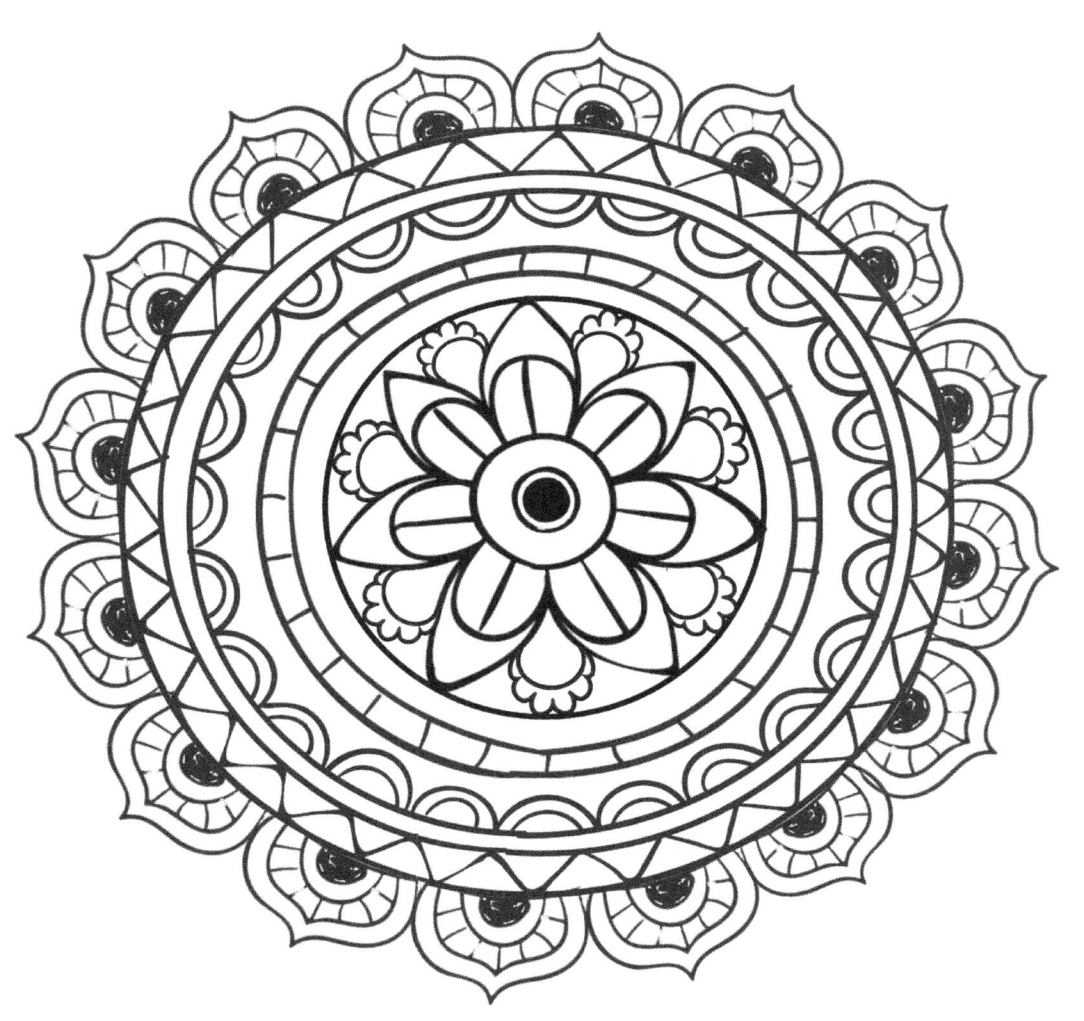

Grass is not always greener on the other side.

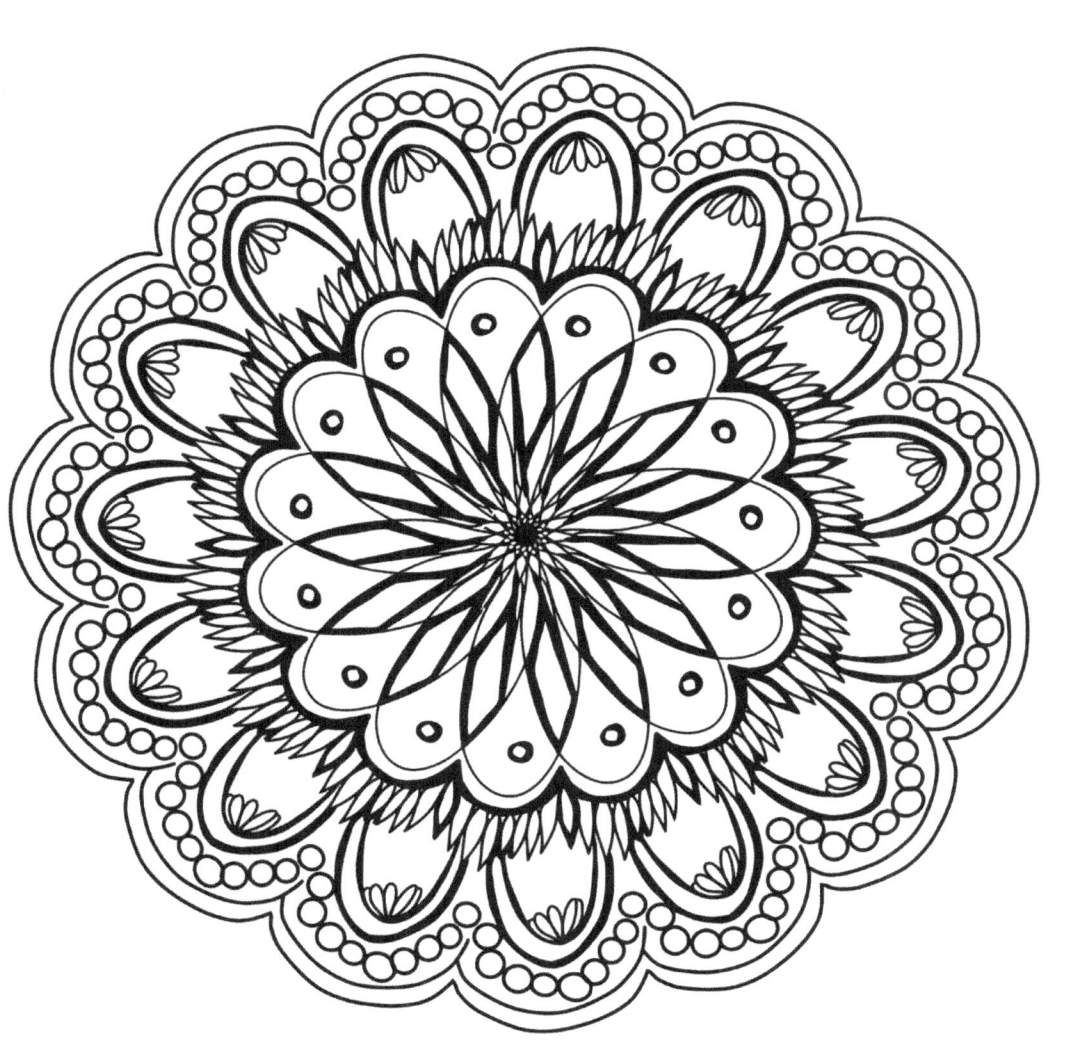

Point to the stars, get to you core.

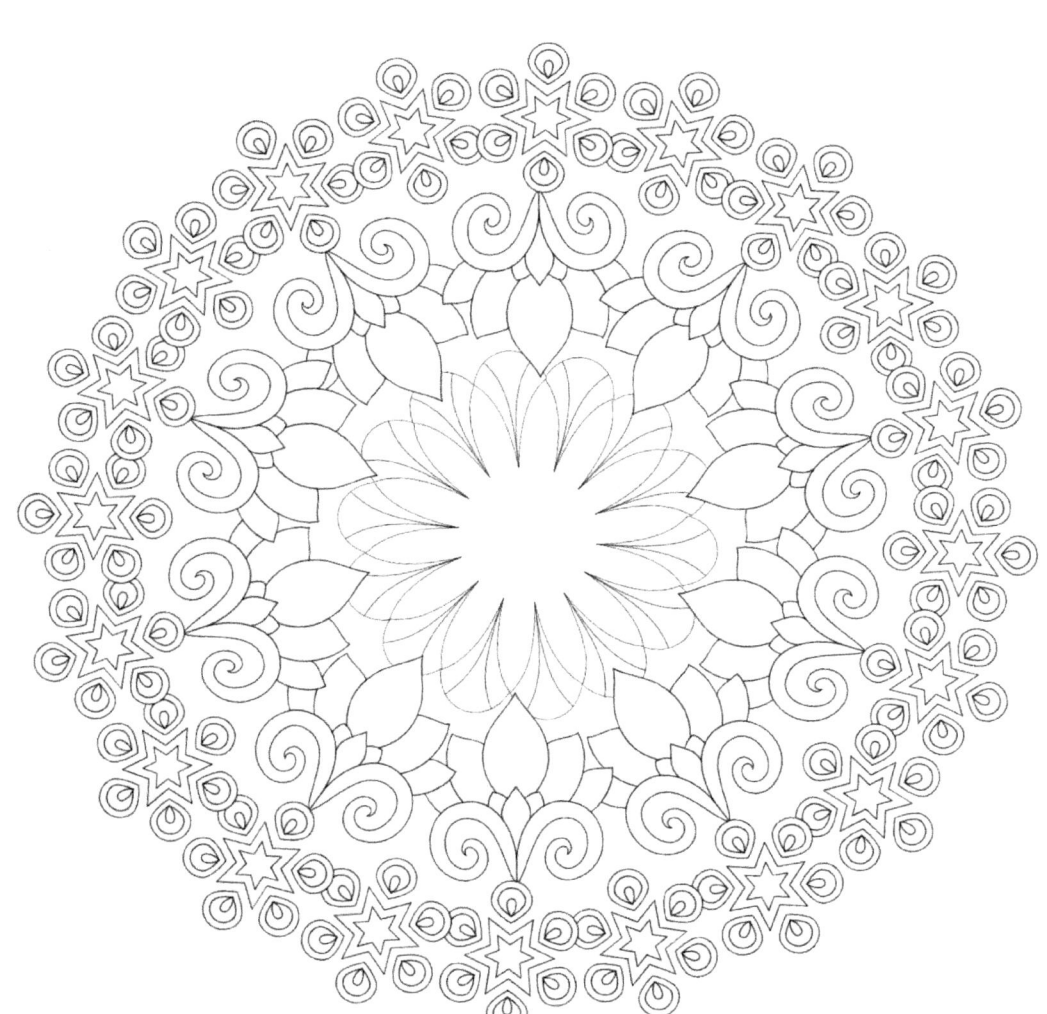

Weave the fabric of your life.

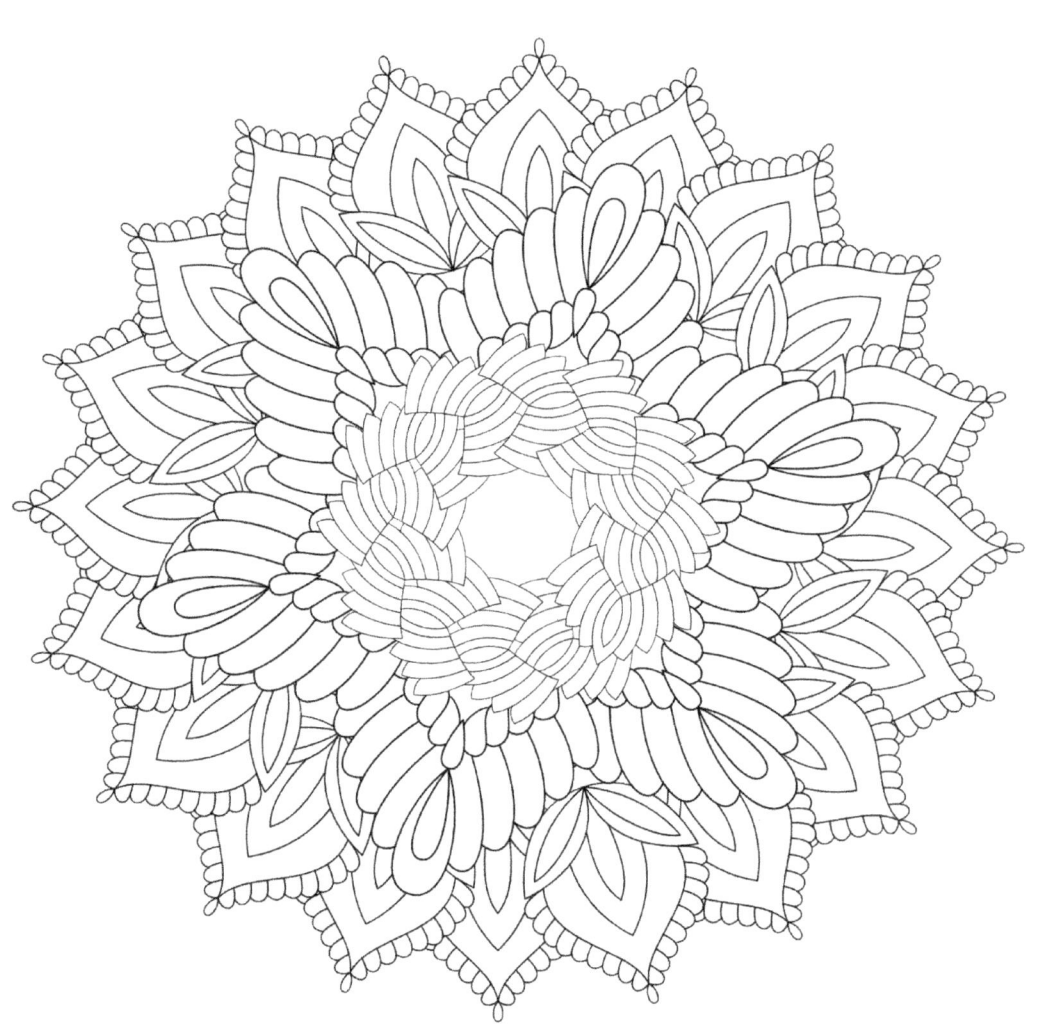

Write down a detailed life plan.

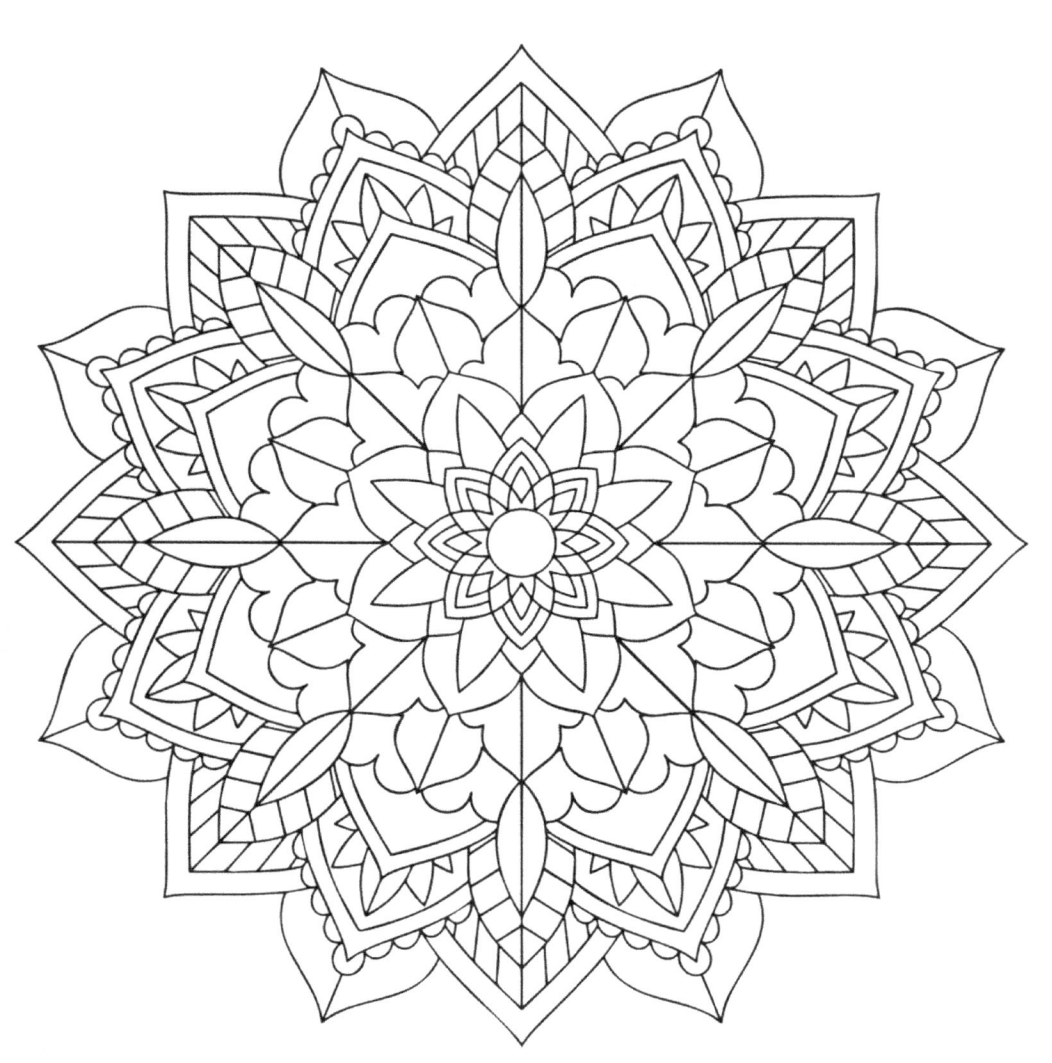

Act, especially when it's not easy.

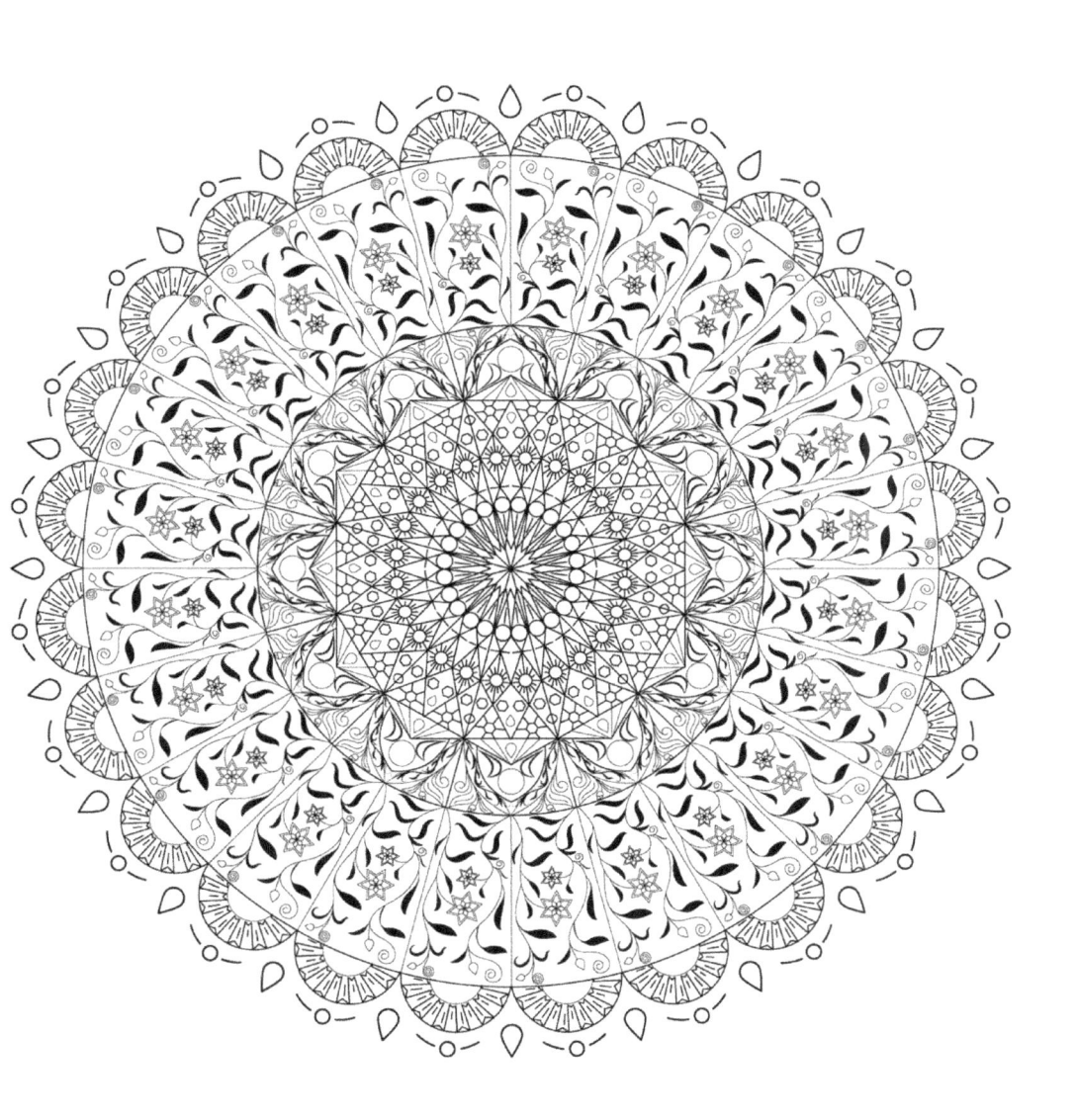

What can you do now to think outside the box?

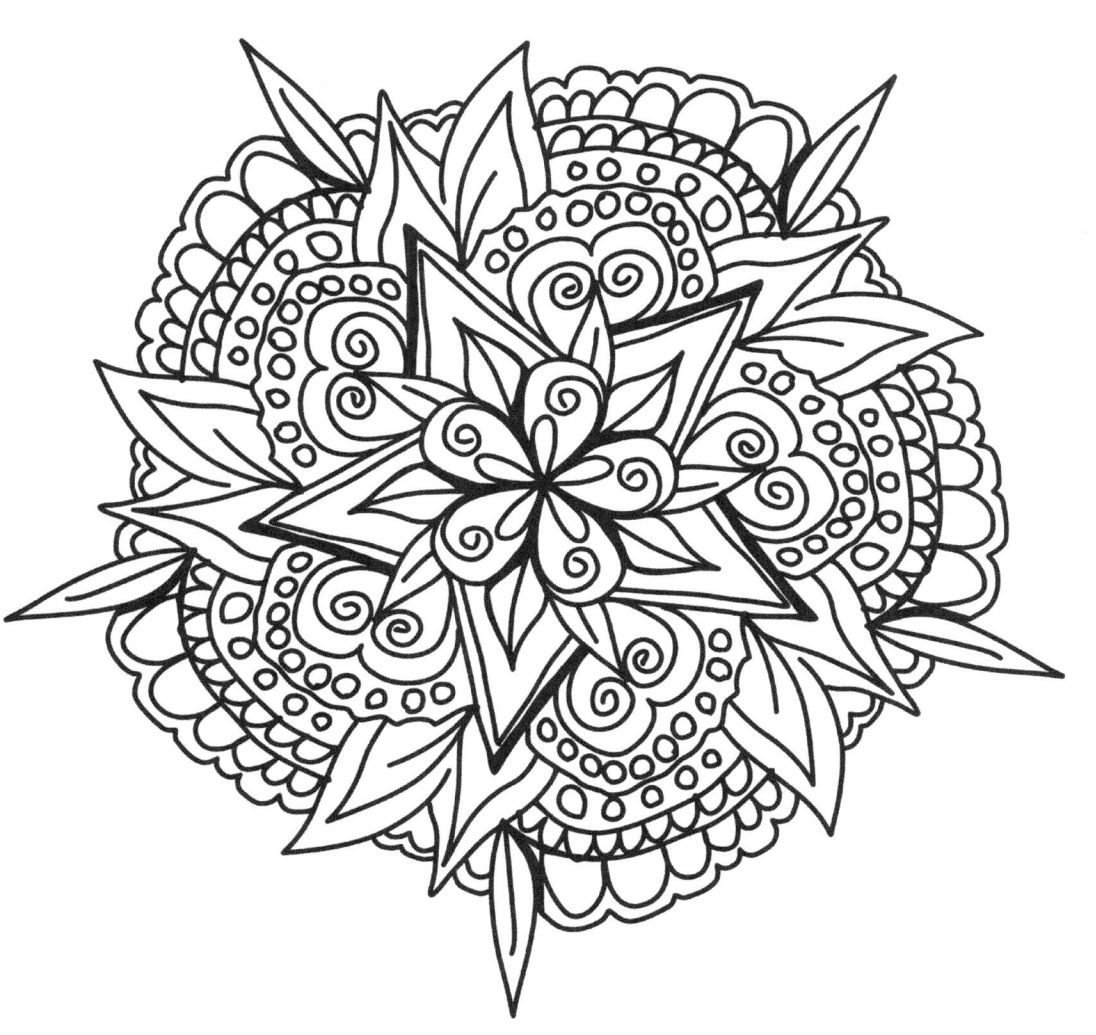

Opportunities and threats are often mixed. Learn to distinguish between them.

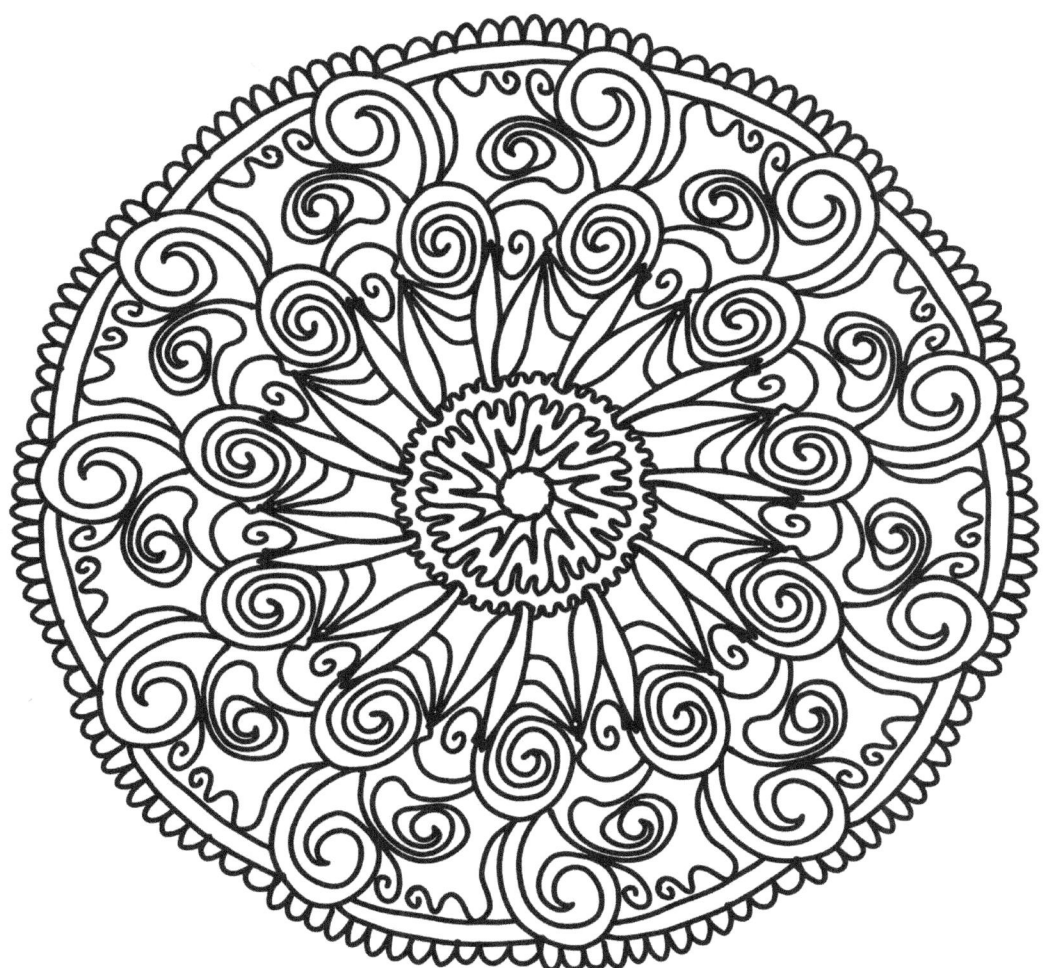

Set high standards.

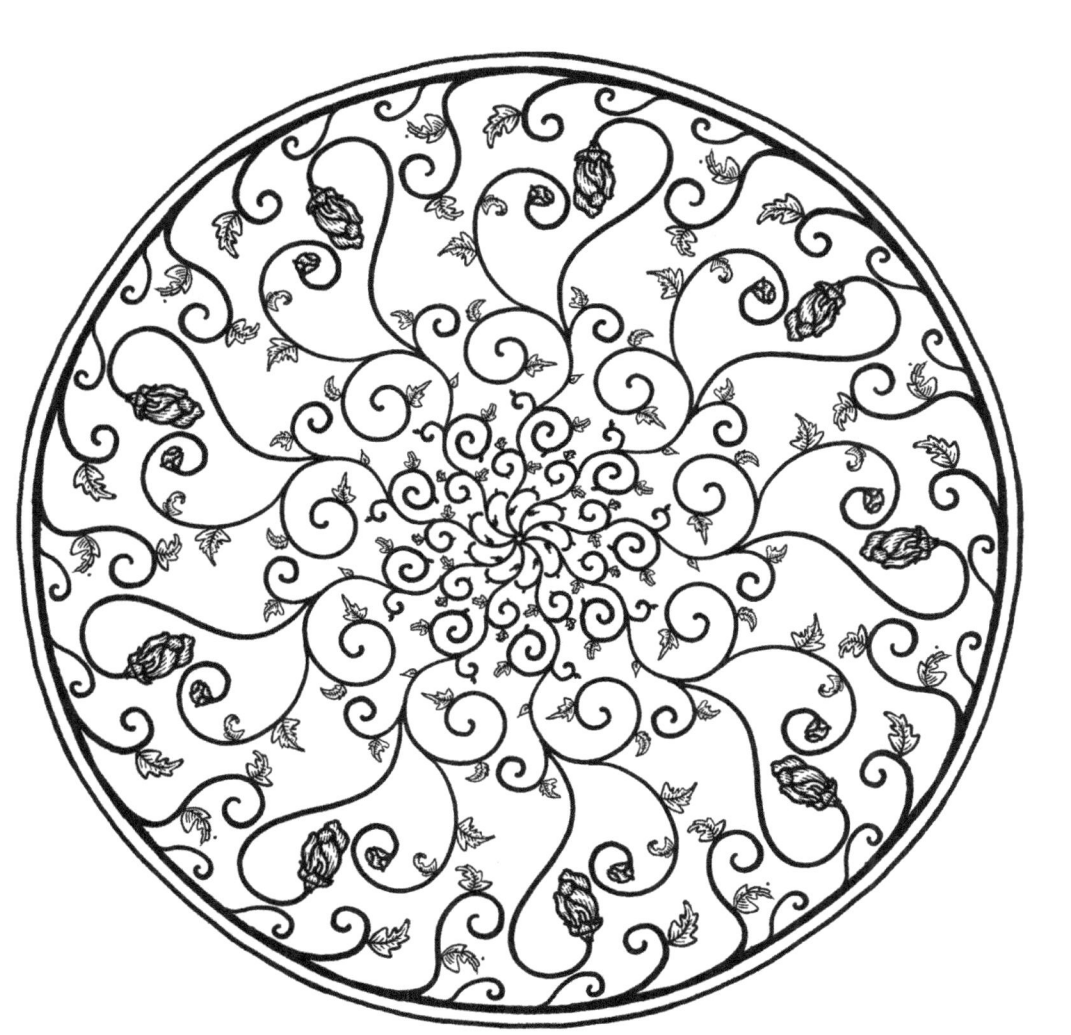

*L*ook into people inside.

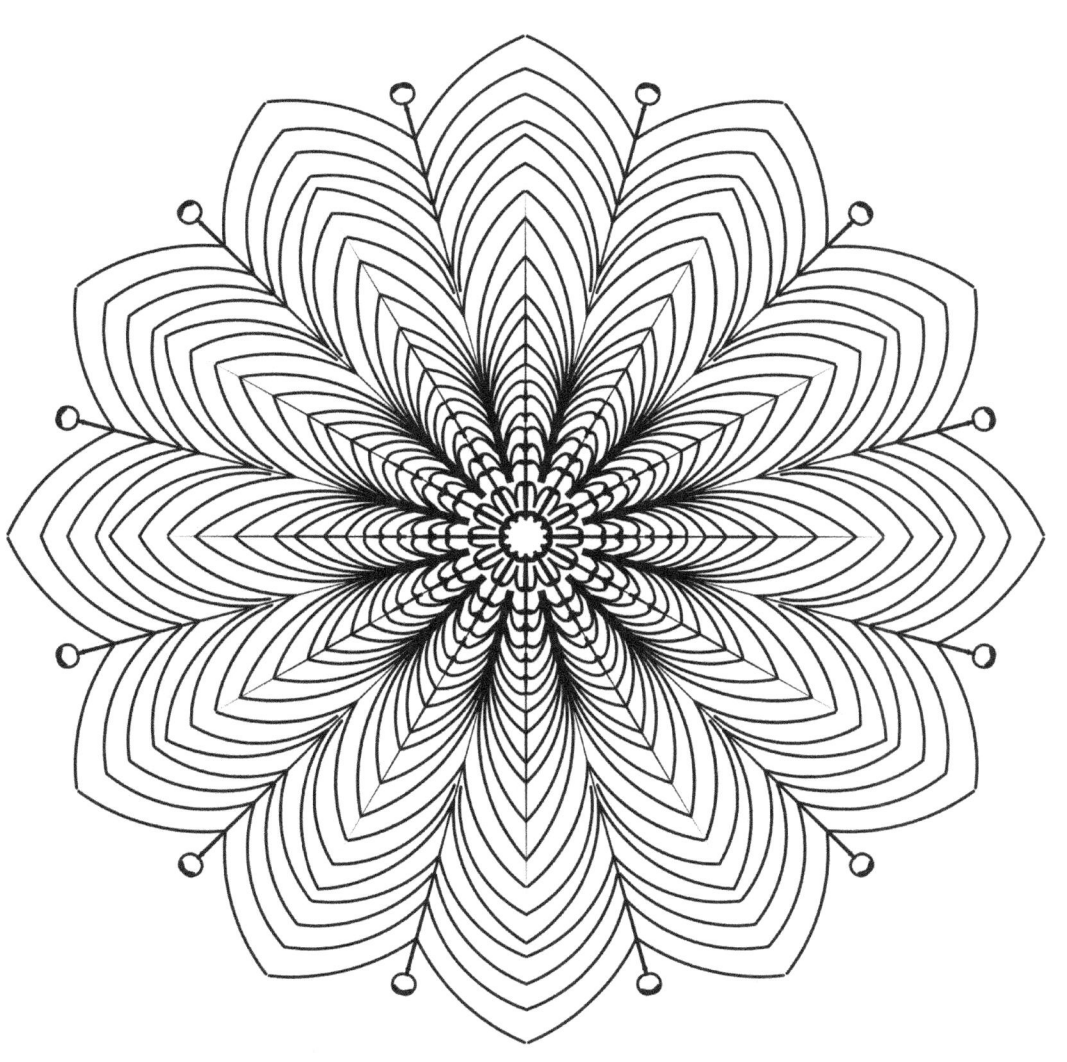

In all directions, flourish.

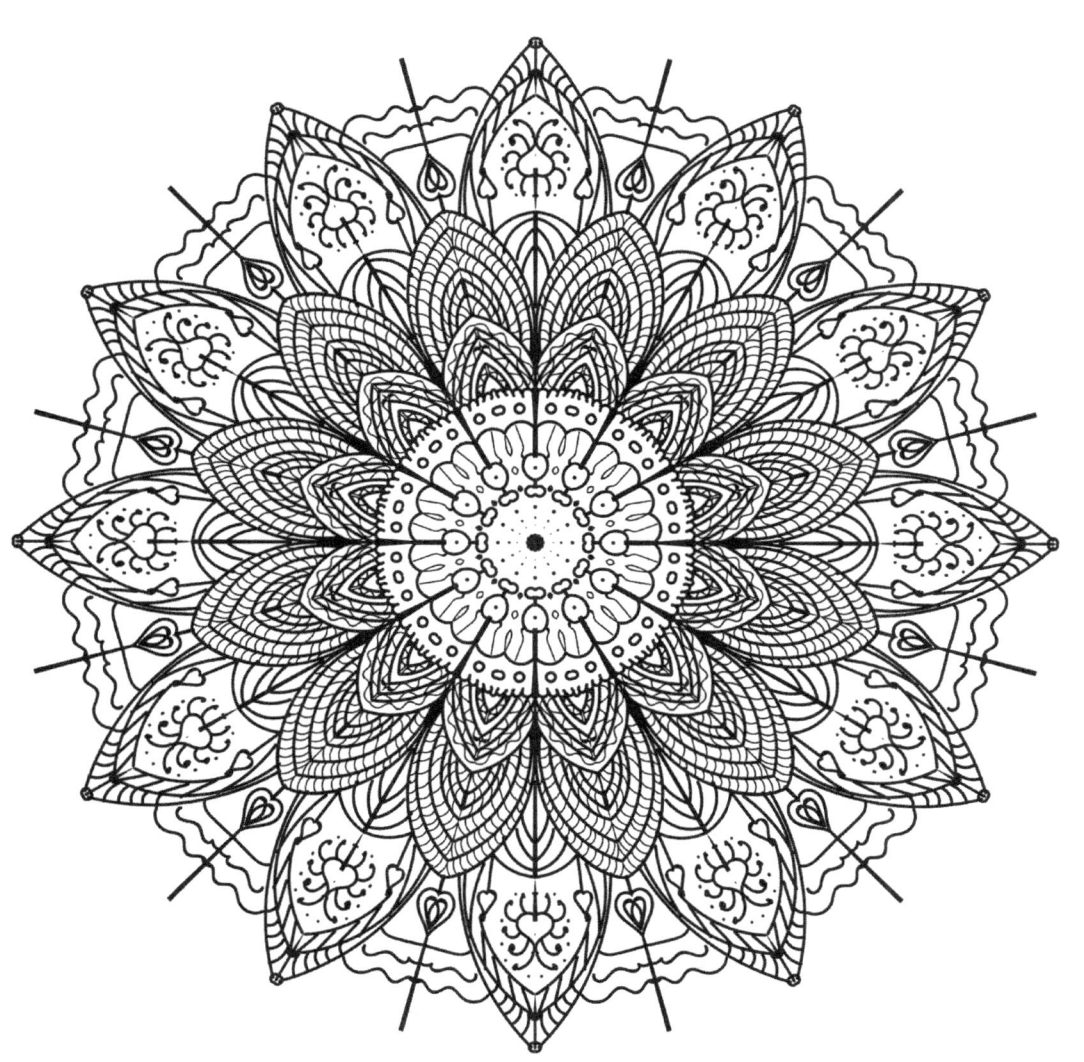

Void is not mere nothingness.

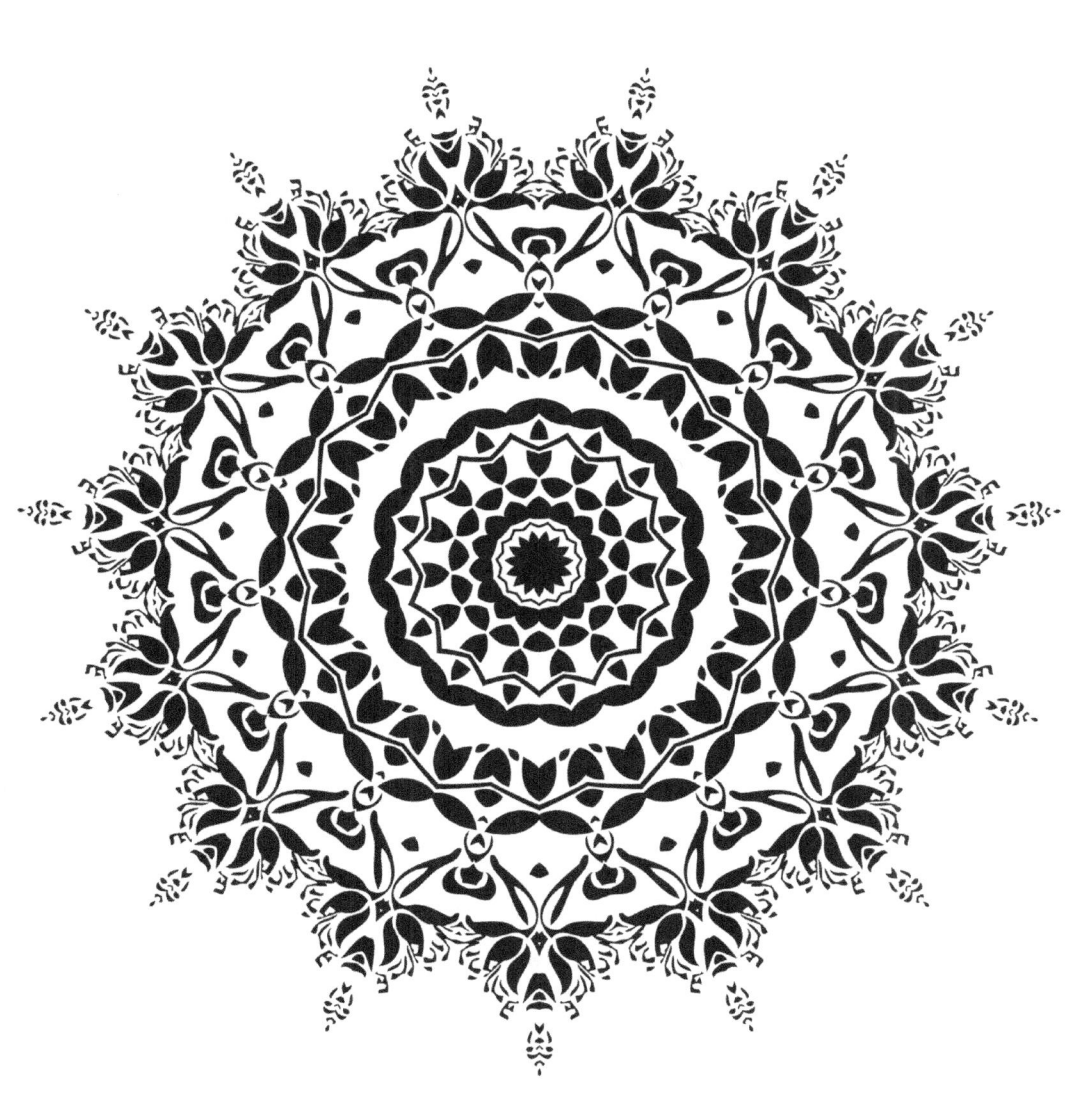

Keep smiling, surprises are around the corner.

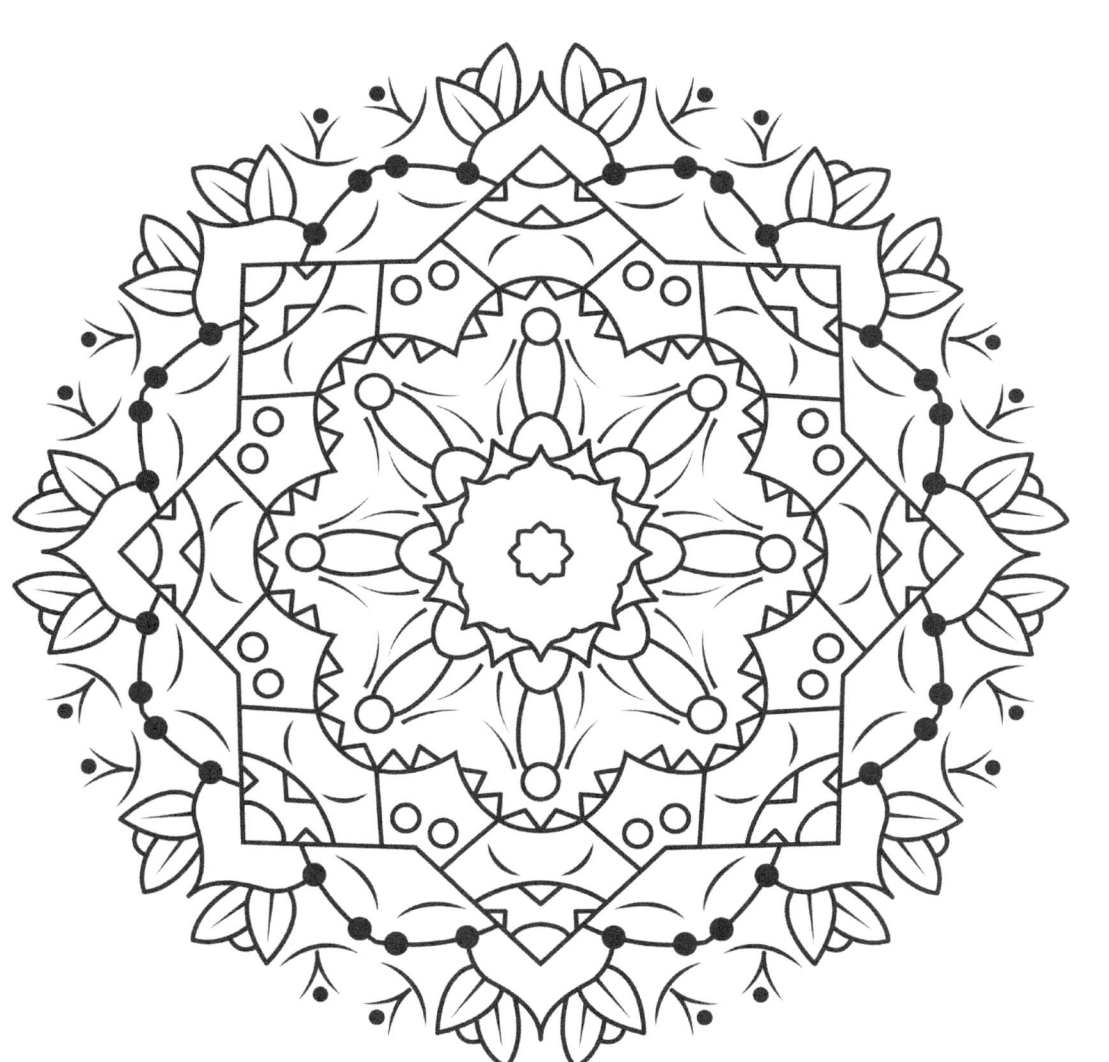

You cannot sharp the universe.

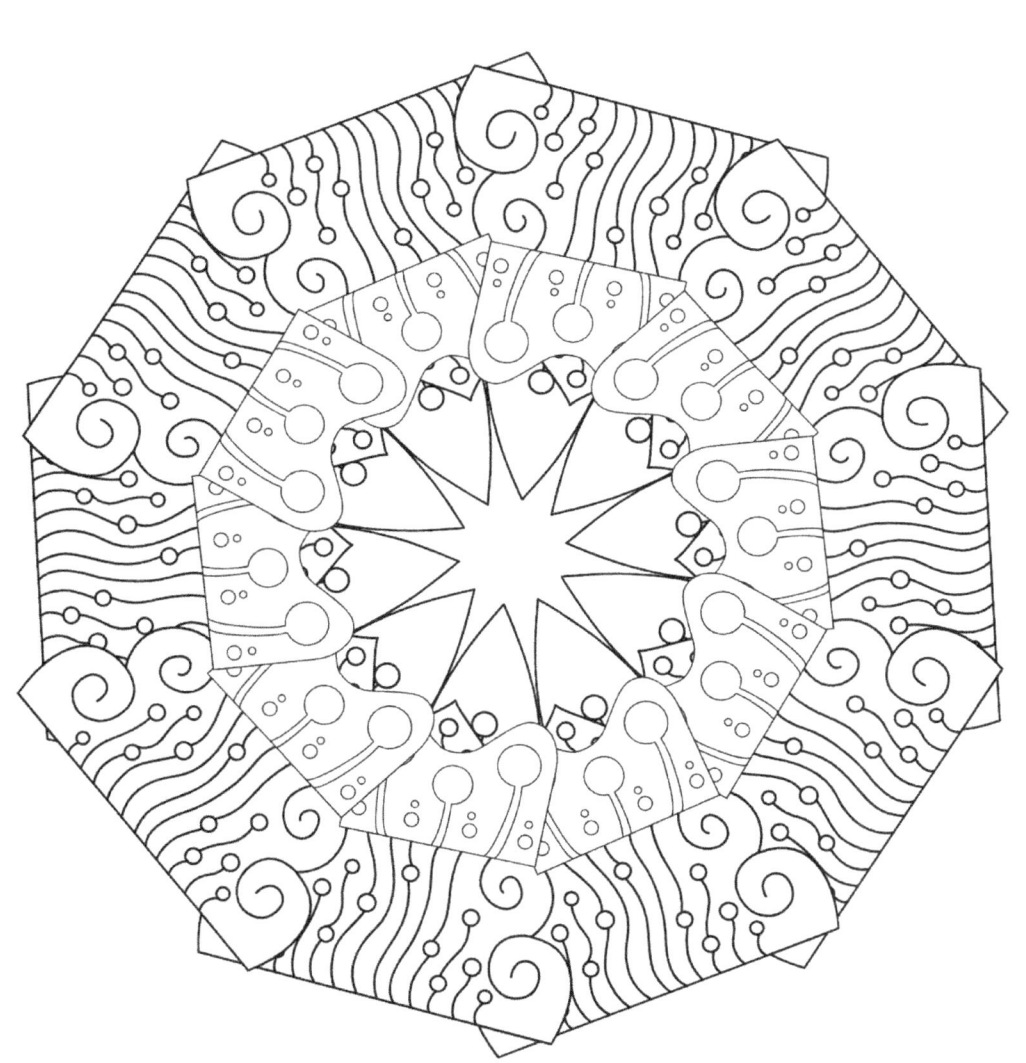

Use a good compass to find the way.

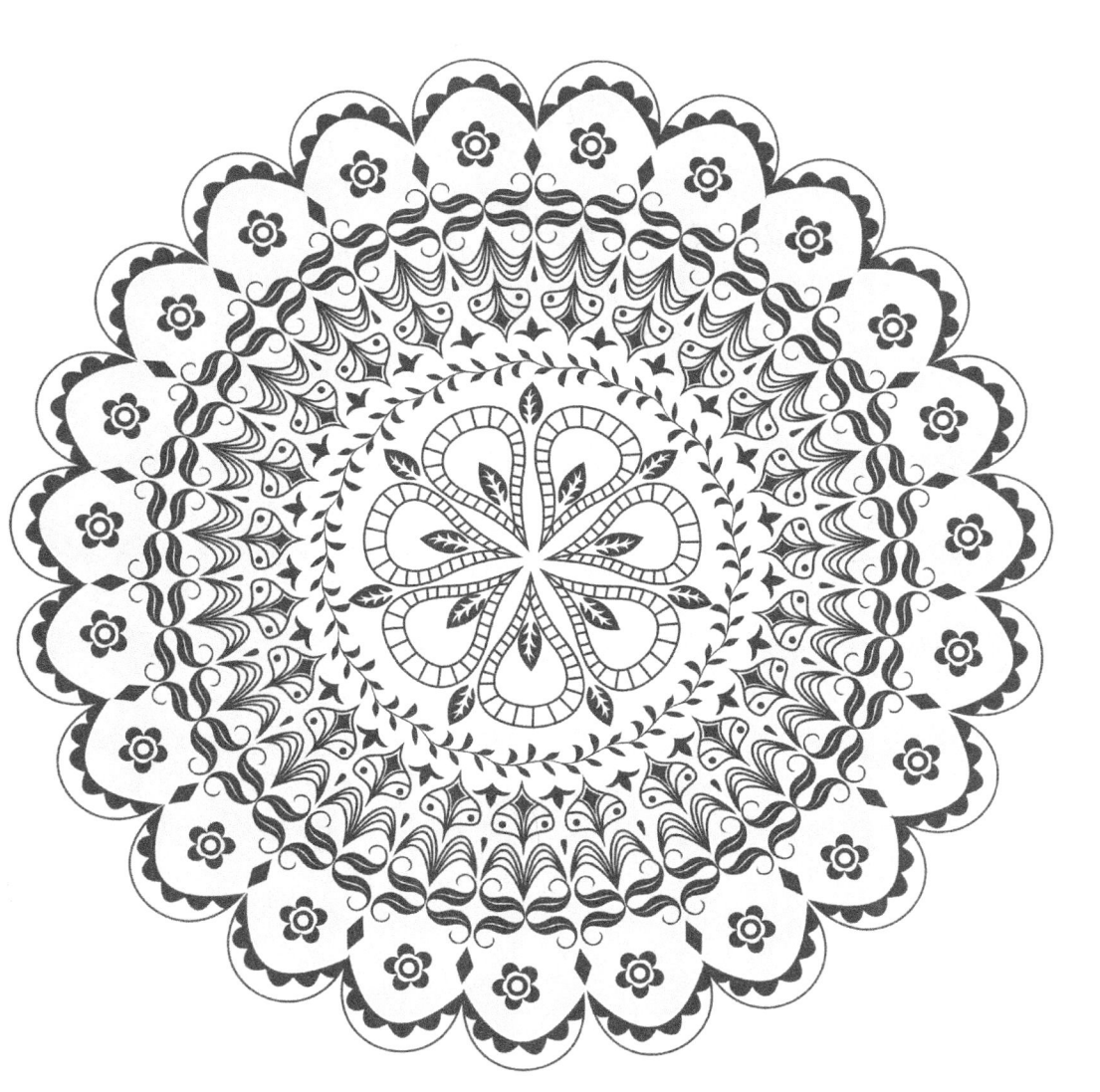

Blossom when it's time.

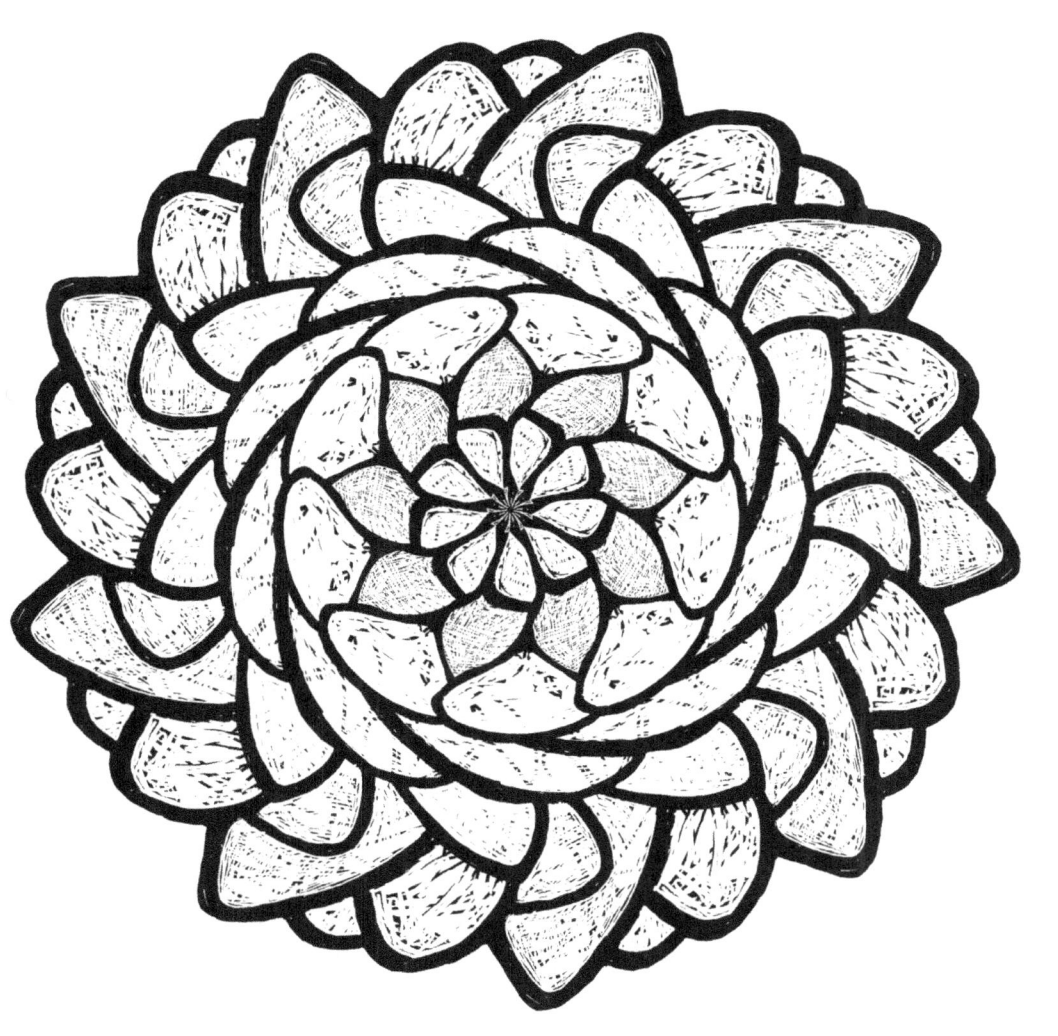

Collect experiences, not objects. They will create a beautiful picture.

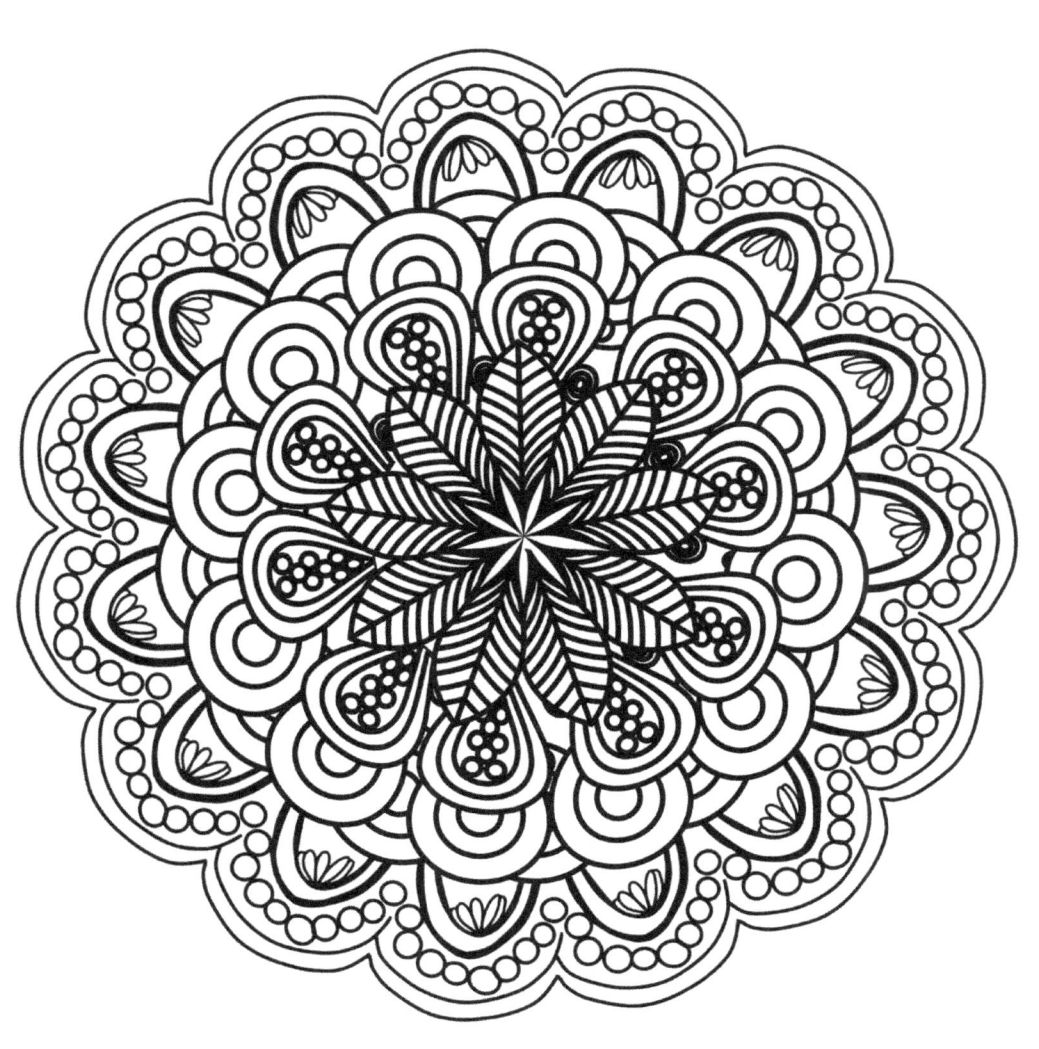

Always shine.

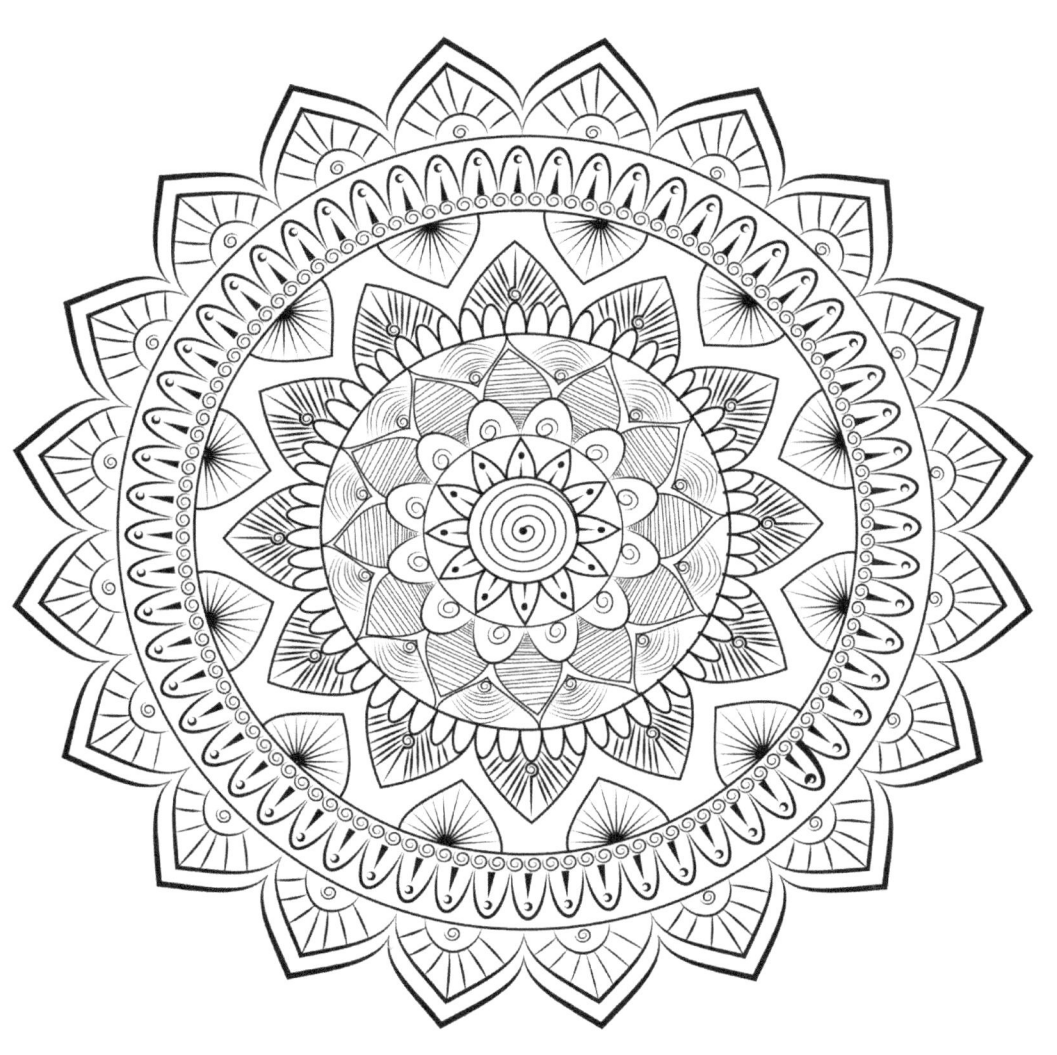

Rights reserved. No written parts of this book nor the cover may be used or reproduced in any manner whatsoever without written permission. The scanning, uploading, and distribution of this book via the internet or via any other means without the permission of the author is illegal.

Purchase only authorized editions of this book and please don't participate in or encourage electronic piracy.

All drawings are open source and credits go to the creators.

First Edition: May 2021

www.ingramcontent.com/pod-product-compliance
Lightning Source LLC
Chambersburg PA
CBHW082016230526
45466CB00022B/2285

IPHONE 15 CAMERA USER GUIDE

"UNLOCKING THE LENS: EXPLORING THE REVOLUTIONARY CAMERA OF THE IPHONE 15"

BY

FRANK SMITH

Copyright © 2024 FRANK SMITH

All rights reserved. This book is copyright and no part of it may be reproduced, distributed, or transmitted in any form or by any means, including photocopying, recording, or other electronic or mechanical methods, without the prior written permission of the publisher, except in the case of brief quotations embodied in critical reviews and certain other noncommercial uses permitted by copyright law.

Printed in the United States of America Copyright 2024

© **FRANK SMITH**